THE BRITISH ISLES

The London Underground
Bakerloo
Central
Circle
District
East London
Hammersmith & City
Jubilee
Metropolitan
Northern
Piccadilly
Victoria
Waterloo & City
DLR
Under construction
National Rail
UNDERGROUND
River Thames
Preston Road
Kingsbury
Brent Cross
Golders Green
Hampstead
Archway
Tufnell Park
Manor House
Tottenham Hale
Walthamstow Central
Wembley Park
Neasden
Dollis Hill
Willesden Green
Kilburn
West Hampstead 200m
Brondesbury Park
Brondesbury
Kensal Rise
Kensal Green
Queen's Park
Finchley Road & Frognal
Belsize Park
Hampstead Heath
Gospel Oak
Kentish Town West
Kentish Town
Chalk Farm
Camden Town
Camden Road
Arsenal
Finsbury Park
Holloway Road
Caledonian Road
Caledonian Road & Barnsbury
Canonbury
Hackney Central
Highbury & Islington
Dalston Kingsland
Homerton
Finchley Road
Swiss Cottage
St. John's Wood
Mornington Crescent
King's Cross St. Pancras
Maida Vale
Kilburn Park
Warwick Avenue
Royal Oak
Westbourne Park
Paddington
Edgware Road
Baker Street
Great Portland Street
Euston
Angel
Warren Street
Euston Square
Euston 200m
Farringdon
Barbican
Old Street
Liverpool Street
Bethnal Green
Mile End
Ladbroke Grove
Latimer Road
White City
Holland Park
Marylebone
Bayswater
Regent's Park
Goodge Street
Russell Square
Moorgate
Shoreditch
Bow Road
Queensway
Lancaster Gate
Bond Street
Oxford Circus
Holborn
Stepney Green
Whitechapel
Aldgate East
All Saints
East Acton
Shepherd's Bush
Notting Hill Gate
Marble Arch
Tottenham Court Road
Chancery Lane
St. Paul's
Bank
Aldgate
High Street Kensington
Hyde Park Corner
Green Park
Covent Garden
Cannon Street
Shadwell
Westferry
Kensington (Olympia)
Piccadilly Circus
Leicester Square
Mansion House
Monument
Tower Hill
Fenchurch Street 150m
Limehouse
Knightsbridge
Charing Cross
Tower Gateway
Goldhawk Road
Hammersmith
Barons Court
Gloucester Road
Sloane Square
St. James's Park
Blackfriars
Wapping
West India Quay
Temple
Rotherhithe
London Bridge
Canary Wharf
West Kensington
Earl's Court
South Kensington
Victoria
Westminster
Embankment
Charing Cross 100m
Bermondsey
Canada Water
Heron Quays
South Quay
West Brompton
Crossharbour & London Arena
Waterloo
Mudchute
Fulham Broadway
Island Gardens
Pimlico
Southwark
Waterloo East
Parsons Green
Lambeth North
Putney Bridge
East Putney
Vauxhall
Elephant & Castle
100m

Let's go 3

von Carl Taylor
sowie Wolfgang Hamm
und Elizabeth Daymond

Herausgeber: Dr. Werner Kieweg, M. A.

Ernst Klett Verlage
Stuttgart · Leipzig

Let's go 3

Im Auftrag des Verlags herausgegeben von:
Dr. Werner Kieweg, M.A., Schwabmünchen

Erarbeitet von:
Carl Taylor, M.A., Maidencombe
sowie
Wolfgang Hamm, Marktredwitz, Elizabeth Daymond, M.A., Kiel

Beratung:
Maria Büse-Dallmann, Unna; Thomas Denk, Karlsruhe;
Ute Fritsch, Ulm; Sibylle Olms, Everswinkel; Ingrid Preedy, Dortmund;
Inge Schott, Sennfeld; Brigitte Seidl, Bochum; Sabine Weingärtner, Schwäbisch Gmünd; Tanja Wiedmann, Lauffen

Visuelle Gestaltung:
Robert Harvey, London; Christian Dekelver, Weinstadt
sowie
Sven Palmowski, Barcelona

Passend zu diesem Band gibt es ein Workbook mit Audio-CD und Lernsoftware (Klettnummer 582638)

1. Auflage

1 5 4 3 2 1 | 2010 09 08 07 06

Alle Drucke dieser Auflage sind unverändert und können im Unterricht nebeneinander verwendet werden. Die letzte Zahl bezeichnet das Jahr des Druckes.

Internetadresse: www.klett.de

Redaktion: Ute Erben, William Sears

Herstellung: Peter Strinz
Umschlagfotos: Mauritius (Merten), Mittenwald;
Avenue Images GmbH (Stockbyte Gold), Hamburg
Reproduktion: Meyle + Müller, Medien-Management, Pforzheim
Druck: J. P. Himmer, Augsburg
Printed in Germany
ISBN-13: 978-3-12-582731-8
ISBN-10: 3-12-582731-0

Hello and welcome to *Let's go 3*!

Let's go 3 besteht aus acht Units. Die Units 1, 3, 5 und 7 sind so aufgebaut, wie du es gewohnt bist: Im Abschnitt **Intro** geht es mit dem Thema der Unit los. Dann kommen die Teile **Language** und **Text** mit einigen kürzeren und einem langen Lesetext. Im Inhaltsverzeichnis siehst du, um was es dabei jeweils geht. Im Teil **Practice** wird geübt und unter **Words** findest du Übungen zu den neuen Wörtern der Unit. Außerdem gibt es hier hilfreiche Tipps zum Umgang mit dem Wörterbuch. In den Teilen **Grammar** und **Let's check** ist noch einmal alles zusammengefasst, was du in der Unit gelernt hast.

Die Units 2, 4, 6 und 8 sind „Kurzunits". Hier gibt es zunächst vier **Topic**-Seiten zum Thema der Unit. Dann folgt unter **Project** eine Projektaufgabe, die du zusammen mit einigen deiner Mitschülerinnen und Mitschüler bearbeiten kannst. Auf der Seite **Let's check** findest du wieder eine Zusammenfassung und außerdem unter **Strategy** viele Tipps zum Training von Hören, Sprechen, Lesen und Schreiben.

Nach den Units 4 und 8 gibt es den Teil **Revision**. Hier kannst du selbstständig üben und wiederholen. Es folgt noch ein Teil **Extra** mit spannenden Infos über Großbritannien und London, Gedichten und Übungen zur Mediation (Vermitteln und Übersetzen).

Wörter, die du nicht mehr weißt, kannst du in der alphabetischen Wortliste ab S. 107 nachschlagen. Danach findest du ganz am Ende eine Liste der unregelmäßigen Verben, die Zahlen, die Lösungen der Revision-Seiten und nützliche Sätze für den Unterricht.

TIPP In den Tipp-Boxen gibt es viele Tipps und Tricks, die das Lernen leichter machen.

Erinnerst du dich noch, was die Zeichen vor Texten und Übungen bedeuten? Hier sind noch einmal die drei wichtigsten:

- (CD) Diese Teile gibt es auch auf der Audio-CD im Workbook.
- **1** (orange) Übungen zum Unit-Inhalt
- **1** (blau) Übungen zum Sprechen, Zusammenarbeiten und Selbermachen

Karneval in London?

Unit 1 London

Intro/	*Hörverstehen*	A temple	8-9
Language	*Sagen, was du regelmäßig machst*	We always go there.	10-11
	Sagen, was du eigentlich tun solltest	We ought to wear nice clothes.	
Text		Let's go to the carnival!	12-13
Practice	*Sprachmittlung: Ein Riesenrad an der Themse*	The London Eye	14-15
Words	*Wortnetz*	In a big city	16-17
	Arbeiten mit dem Wörterbuch I		
Grammar	*Einfache Gegenwart: Verwendung und Bildung*	present simple	18
	Modale Hilfsverben	ought to, must, mustn't	
Let's check	*London*		19
	Ein Witz	Two camels	

Wir telefonieren!

Unit 2 It's good to talk!

Topic	*Ein Telefongespräch führen*	It's me. Can we talk?	20-23
	Sagen, was man mit einem Handy tun sollte	People should switch off their phones on trains.	
	Hörverstehen mit DJ Dan	In Devon	
Project	*Kommunikation früher und heute: Eine Ausstellung oder eine Präsentation*	Communication	24
Let's check/	*Handys*		25
Strategy	*Lernstrategien: Lesen*	Reading	

Unit 3 Wales

Verliebt in Wales

Intro/ Language	*Hörverstehen*	Katja und Kerry	26-27
	Über Vergangenes sprechen	Did you forget the training? – No, I didn't. I saw her again yesterday.	28-29
	Sagen, auf welche Art und Weise etwas geschehen ist	She read the message carefully.	
Text		Katja and Rhodri	30-31
Practice	*Sprachmittlung: Im Fußballclub*	At the Abergavenny football club	32-33
Words	*Wortnetz*	Sports and music	34-35
	Arbeiten mit dem Wörterbuch II		
Grammar	*Vergangenheit: Verwendung und Bildung*	past simple	36
	Adjektive und Adverbien	adjectives and adverbs	
Let's check	*Wales*		37
	Optische Täuschungen	Two tricks	

Unit 4 Is school cool?

Stress in der Schule

Topic	*Über die Schule sprechen*	I've tried to work harder this year.	38-41
	Über Regeln und Strafen sprechen	We mustn't eat in the classroom.	
	Hörverstehen mit DJ Dan	Four pupils	
Project	*Mobbing in der Schule*	Bullying	42
Let's check/ Strategy	*Schule*		43
	Lernstrategien: Schreiben	Writing	

Revision 1-4	*Üben und wiederholen*	Grammar, words	44-45

Ein Monster im See?

Unit 5 Scotland

Intro/	*Hörverstehen*	Two holidays	46-47
Language	*Sagen, was jemand gerade gemacht hat*	She has just ordered breakfast.	48-49
	Fragen, ob jemand etwas schon erledigt hat	Have you booked your boat trip yet?	
	Fragen, wo jemand schon einmal gewesen ist	Have you ever been to Berlin?	
Text		A photo of Nessie?	50-51
Practice	*Sprachmittlung: In einer Jugendherberge*	In a youth hostel	52-53
Words	*Wortnetz*	Nature	54-55
	Arbeiten mit dem Wörterbuch III		
Grammar	*Perfekt: Verwendung und Bildung*	present perfect	56
Let's check	*Schottland*		57
	Ein Banküberfall geht schief	A bad idea!	

Mit Musik geht alles besser!

Unit 6 My music

Topic	*Über musikalische Vorlieben sprechen*	Music is important for me. But I don't like jazz.	58-61
	Etwas genauer beschreiben	I like the clothes that they wear.	
	Hörverstehen mit DJ Dan	Young people and music	
Project	*Ein Bandprofil erstellen*	Profile of a band	62
Let's check/	*Musik*		63
Strategy	*Lernstrategien: Sprechen*	Speaking	

Unit 7 Crazy weather

Unwetter mit Folgen

Intro/ Language	*Hörverstehen*	The weather report	64-65
	Sagen, was ich unter Bedingungen machen werde	If it rains tomorrow, I won't stay here.	66-67
	Sagen, was ich selbst mache	I always tidy up myself.	
Text		The storm	68-69
Practice	*Sprachmittlung: Verhalten im Brandfall*	Fire	70-71
Words	*Wortnetz*	Weather	72-73
	Arbeiten mit dem Wörterbuch IV		
Grammar	*Bedingungssätze*	if-clauses	74
	Reflexivpronomen	reflexive pronouns	
Let's check	*Wetter*		75
	Wasser sparen im Hotel	Help us to help the environment!	

Unit 8 Top sports

Welcher Sporttyp bist du?

Topic	*Über verschiedene Sportarten sprechen*	I don't think that's a sport.	76-79
		I prefer to be active.	
	Einen Text auswerten	Active type or couch potato?	
	Hörverstehen mit DJ Dan	Which sports?	
Project	*Ein Vereinsprofil erstellen*	Sports clubs	80
Let's check/	*Sport*		81
Strategy	*Lernstrategien: Hörverstehen*	Listening	
Revision 5-8	*Üben und wiederholen*	Grammar, words	82-83

Extra

Mediation	*Sprachmittlung*		84-85
One country – or four?	*Das Vereinigte Königreich*		86
A dangerous place	*London vor 400 Jahren*		87
Andrew's photos	*Urlaubsfotos*		88-89
Three poems	*Gedichte*		90
Vocabulary	*Hinweise zum Vokabular*		91
	Englische Laute, das Alphabet		
	Chronologische Wortliste		92
Alphabetical word list	*Alphabetische Wortliste*	English-German	107-120
		German-English	121-130
Check the answers!	*Lösungen der* Revision-*Seiten*		131
Irregular verbs	*Unregelmäßige Verben,*		132-133
Numbers	*Zahlen*		
In the classroom	*Wendungen für den Unterricht*	Can I print it out?	134-135

London

a

The Notting Hill Carnival is during the last weekend in August. The first carnival was in 1964. It was just a street party. Today it's a very big event. Over two million people take part every year.

The Notting Hill Carnival is fun. I go every year with my parents. You can dance and listen to the music. We always watch the processions.

I've got an uncle in America. He stays with us every summer. He always wants to see the same sights. It's so boring. How often can you look at Buckingham Palace?

The Tower of London is a very old castle. It was the home of kings and queens for hundreds of years. Buckingham Palace is the Queen's home in London now. Today, tourists can visit the palace and the tower.

The Tower of London

1 London is a great city!

Find out.

1. Why does Terry like the Notting Hill Carnival?
2. Why is it so boring for Sam when his uncle is in London?
3. Why is Emma so excited?
4. Why is shopping in London so awesome for Lisa?

2 Speaking: Interesting sights

Make dialogues with a partner.

A: What would you like to do in London?
B: I'd like to visit the Tower of London.
A: Why?
B: Because I like castles.

…

It could be fun. I've never seen … .
I like … . I think … . …

The Hindu temple is in North London. It's the largest Hindu temple in Europe. Every year 50,000 people go to Hindu festivals there.

Most tourists go to Oxford Street, in the West End. The most famous shops are there.

3 Listening: A temple

Some tourists are visiting the Hindu temple. *Listen and take notes.*

1. The temple opened in … .
2. The parts for the temple came from … .
3. People worked for … years to make the temple in London.
4. … schools have visited the temple.
5. … people have visited the temple.

4 More about London

a) *Make a list of sights in London.*

b) *Find information about one of the sights. You can look in the library or on the internet. Then tell the class.*

- What's the name of the sight?
- Where is it?
- What can you do / see there?

b Sam's uncle, Fred, visits London every summer. He's sent an e-mail.

Mr Spencer: Can you show Fred the Tower of London, Sam?
Sam: The Tower of London? Again? We always do that with Fred.
Mr Spencer: Have you got any good ideas?
Sam: I can show him the London Eye.
Mr Spencer: I think he'll enjoy that.
Sam: Does he like music?
Mr Spencer: Yes, he does.
Sam: I'll take him to the Notting Hill Carnival, too. The bands play great music there. And it's free.
Mr Spencer: When does the carnival start?
Sam: On Sunday. Terry always goes there. We can meet him.

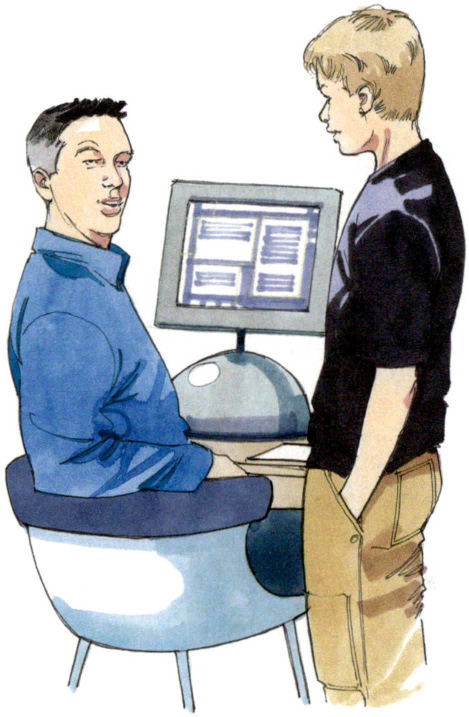

Say it!

We always **do** that.	*Das **machen** wir immer.*
Terry always **goes** there.	*Terry **geht** immer dorthin.*

5 A visit from America

What's missing? play goes visits do likes wants starts

1. Fred … London every summer.
2. Sam and Fred always … the same things.
3. Sam … to go to the London Eye.
4. Fred … music.
5. The bands … great music at the carnival.
6. The carnival … on Sunday.
7. Terry always … to the carnival.

6 Speaking: Have you got any good ideas?

a) *Think about the places and activities in your town. Make two lists.*

interesting ☺	boring ☹
leisure centre …	park …

b) *Make dialogues with a partner. Use your lists.*

A: My cousin wants to visit me. What can we do? Have you got any good ideas?
B: You can show her ☹. She'll like that.
A: That's boring. We always do that.
B: Well, you could show her ☺.
A: That's a good idea.

That's cool.
He'll/She'll enjoy that.
…

That's awful.
I hate that.
…

c Lisa is at home. She's got her mobile phone.

Lisa: Hello?
Emma: Hi, Lisa, it's Emma. Would you like to come to the wedding on Saturday? We can go together.
Lisa: That's so cool. I've never seen a Hindu wedding. Can I wear my new sweatshirt?
Emma: No, you can't. We ought to wear Indian clothes. I can give you some.
Lisa: Thanks. Is the wedding in the temple?
Emma: No, it isn't. There aren't any weddings in the temple. But it's near the temple. We must leave my house at nine o'clock. We mustn't be late. And we ought to visit the temple, too.
Lisa: OK.

Say it!

We **ought to wear** Indian clothes.
*Wir **sollten eigentlich** indische Kleidung **tragen**.*

7 An Indian wedding

Make sentences.

can't wear | mustn't be | ought to visit | can go | can give | ought to wear | must leave

1. Lisa and Emma/to the wedding
   Lisa and Emma can go to the wedding.
2. Lisa/her new sweatshirt
   Lisa can't … . *Go on, please.*
3. Lisa and Emma/Indian clothes
4. Emma/Lisa some clothes
5. They/Emma's house at nine o'clock
6. They/late for the wedding
7. The girls/the Hindu temple

8 Speaking: Special clothes

1

come to a wedding/ Saturday

2

play in a football game/ tomorrow

3

help me in the garden/ Sunday

Make dialogues with a partner.

1. *A:* Hi, would you like to come to a wedding on Saturday?
   B: That's cool.
   A: You ought to wear your best clothes.
   B: OK. I've got … .
2. *Go on, please.*

your best clothes
a red T-shirt
old clothes/jeans
a nice shirt/dress
…

Let's go to the carnival!

It was the last weekend in August. Sam and his uncle were at the London Eye. Now Uncle Fred wanted to visit the Tower of London and then Buckingham Palace.

"We go there every year," said Sam.
"I love it," said Fred. "We haven't got a Queen in America."
"My friend Terry is at the Notting Hill Carnival. We should go there. It'll be fun. People dance and play music. You can eat West Indian food."
"OK," said Fred. "We can go to the Tower of London tomorrow."

Sam decided to take the Underground to Oxford Circus and change to the Central Line. There were lots of people on the train. The train left the station and went into a tunnel. Then it stopped.

"What's the problem?" asked Fred.
"This often happens," said Sam.
But then suddenly it was very dark.
"What do we do now?" asked Fred.
"How long will we be here?"
"I don't know," said Sam.
Sam took his mobile phone. "Look. I can use my phone like a torch."
Other people took their mobile phones. They used them like torches in the dark train.
They waited and waited. It was now very hot.

Then suddenly the train started and they came out of the tunnel.
They came to the next station. The doors opened. A voice said loudly, "Please get off the train. There is a problem in the tunnel."
Sam and his uncle came out of the Underground station.
"That was awful," said Fred. "Let's take a taxi. I don't want to sit in another dark tunnel."

Fred saw a black London taxi. He opened the door and they jumped in.
"Notting Hill Gate, please," said Sam.
"You can't drive there today," said the driver. "It's the carnival."
They climbed out of the taxi.
"Uncle Fred, quick," said Sam. "A bus is coming. It goes to Notting Hill Gate."
Sam and Fred jumped into the bus. They bought two tickets. The bus went slowly along thc road.

"I think we'll go to Piccadilly Circus," said Sam. "And along Oxford Street."
Fred looked at the sights. But suddenly the bus stopped.
"What's happening now?" asked Fred.
Sam went to the driver. When he came back, he said, "There's a demonstration near Trafalgar Square."
"OK," said Fred. "That's that. Let's walk. Have you got a map?"
"Yes," said Sam.
"May I see it?"
They got off the bus and started to walk.

After one hour, they arrived in Notting Hill. They heard music and saw dancers in the streets.
"Does Terry know that we want to meet him?" asked Fred. "You ought to phone him."
"OK." Sam took his mobile phone.
"Oh, no," he said. "I've got no credit."
"This is crazy," said Fred. "Haven't you got a meeting place?"
Then Sam's phone rang. It was Terry.
"Hi, Terry," said Sam. "Yes, we're in front of the Café Mambo. Where are you?"
Then Fred heard Terry's voice.
"I'm behind you, Sam," said Terry.
"You don't need your phone."

1 Where were Sam and Fred?

What's the right order?

In the taxi | In Notting Hill | On the bus

In front on the café | On the Underground | At the London Eye

1. 'At the London Eye' is first.
2. … . *Go on, please.*

2 Fred's story

Fred sent an e-mail to a friend in America. *What did he say?*

Dear Charles,
I was in London with Sam yesterday. First we went to the London Eye. That was really interesting. Then we decided to go to the Notting Hill Carnival.
First we took the ... . But then it stopped. ...

1 An interesting job

In the summer Louise works in the Tower of London. *Talk about her day.*

1

go to work / by Underground

2

start work / 9.30

3

talk to tourists / about the tower

4

tell stories / about kings and queens

5
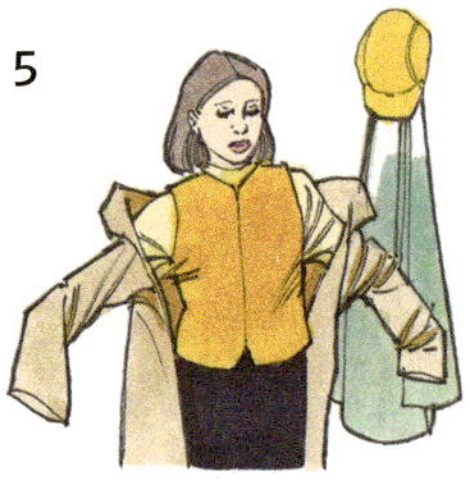
finish work / 5.30

6

arrive home / 7.00

1. Louise goes to work by Underground. 2. She starts … . *Go on, please.*

2 A trip to London

You want to book a trip to London. *What's the right question?*

1. *Du möchtest wissen, wie viel ein Flug nach London kostet.*
   a) How much does a flight to London cost?
   b) How many planes go to London?
2. *Du möchtest die Abflugszeit wissen.*
   a) Where does the plane leave?
   b) When does the plane leave?
3. *Du möchtest wissen, wo das Flugzeug landet.*
   a) When does the plane land?
   b) Where does the plane land?
4. *Du möchtest wissen, wie du in die Innenstadt kommst.*
   a) How do we go from the airport to London?
   b) How do we go from London to the airport?
5. *Du möchtest wissen, wie viel ein U-Bahn-Ticket kostet.*
   a) Where can I get an Underground ticket?
   b) How much does an Underground ticket cost?
6. *Du möchtest jemanden fragen, ob es billige Hotels gibt.*
   a) Do you know any cheap hotels?
   b) How much is the cheapest hotel?

3 Listening: London can be cheap!

A German family is at a London Tourist Information Centre. They think London is expensive. The woman is telling them about some free activities.
Listen and make a list of free activities.

Free activities in London

the British Museum
the …

4 Carnival tips

Match the parts of the sentences.

1. All the roads in Notting Hill are closed on the day of the carnival. You mustn't
2. You ought to
3. It's difficult to meet friends without a mobile phone. You ought to
4. West Indian food is great! You ought to
5. Remember, it's summer! You must
6. You must be careful

drink lots of water.
try some at the carnival.
with wallets and money at the carnival.
drive.
take one.
take the Underground to Notting Hill.

5 Speaking: On the Underground

You're at Paddington Station and you want to go to one of the places in this unit.
Look at the Underground map at the front of the book. Make dialogues with a partner.

A: I'd like to see Big Ben. How can we go there?
B: We can take the Circle Line from here to Baker Street. Then we change to the Bakerloo Line. We get off at Westminster.

Place	Underground
1. Big Ben	Westminster
2. Buckingham Palace	Green Park
3. Trafalgar Square	Charing Cross
4. Science Museum	South Kensington
5. Tower of London	Tower Hill

6 Mediation: The London Eye

You're in London with your class. You're at the London Eye. Two German people want to book a trip on the Eye.
Can you help them?

Woman: Good morning. What can I do for you?
Mr Fiebig: Sage, dass wir gerne Fahrkarten für das ‚London Eye' kaufen wollen.
You: These people would like to …
Woman: I'm sorry, they must wait for two hours. I haven't got any tickets now.
You: …
Mrs Fiebig: Können wir Karten für morgen kaufen?
You: …
Woman: Yes. The first trip is at half past nine. Tickets are £12.
You: …
Mr Fiebig: Können wir bitte zwei Karten für morgen früh haben?
You: …
Woman: Yes, they can. That's £24, please.
You: …

TIPP

Arbeiten mit dem Wörterbuch I

Wenn du etwas auf Englisch nicht sagen kannst, weil dir ein Wort fehlt, dann kannst du im **deutsch-englischen** Teil deines Wörterbuchs nachschauen, z. B.

Is there a "Jugendherberge" near here?

> **Jugendherberge** youth hostel
> **jugendlich** ❶ (*jung*) young ❷ (*jung wirkend*) youthful

Wenn du die deutsche Bedeutung eines englischen Wortes nicht weißt, dann schaust du im **englisch-deutschen** Teil deines Wörterbuchs nach, z. B.

We've got lots of youth hostels here in Britain.

> **youth hostel** Jugendherberge
> **you've** [ju:v] *Kurzform von* **you have**
> **Yu·go·sla·via** [ˈju:gəʊˈslɑ:vɪə] Jugoslawien

In einem Wörterbuch sind Wörter nicht nur nach ihren Anfangsbuchstaben geordnet, sondern auch nach den nachfolgenden Buchstaben, z. B.
about – accident – address – adventure – after

1. In welcher Reihenfolge stehen die folgenden Wörter im Wörterbuch? Schreibe die Lösung auf ein Blatt Papier.
   street – bus – famous – temple – wedding – Underground – change – unit
2. Und in welcher Reihenfolge findest du die folgenden Wörter? Schreibe die Lösung ebenfalls auf ein Blatt Papier.
   sweatshirt – sea – sad – skateboard – smelly – strange – suddenly – spicy
3. Schreibe nun einige Wörter aus dem Wörterbuch heraus, verändere ihre Reihenfolge und lege sie dann deinem Partner zur Lösung vor.

7 Word web: In a big city

a) *Make a word web for 'in a big city' in your exercise book. You can also use a dictionary.*

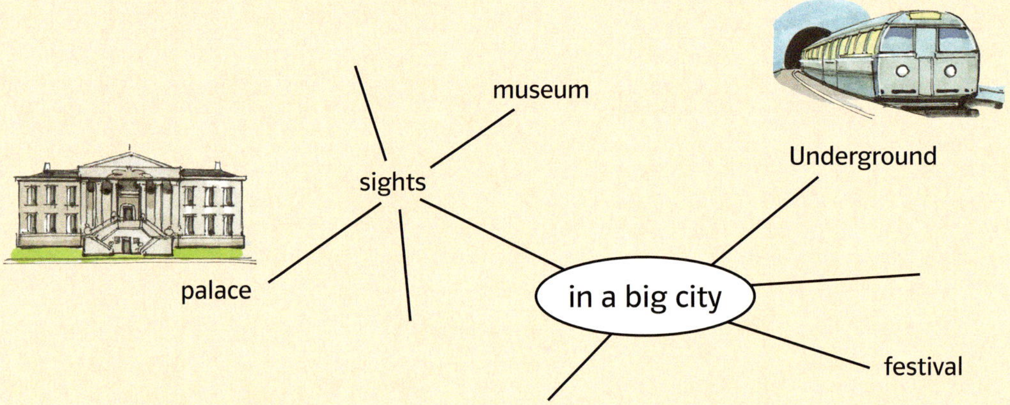

b) *Which things in the word web have you got in your city, town or village?*

My town has got a … but there isn't a … . We've got … .
Go on, please.

8 Listen and speak

[i:]

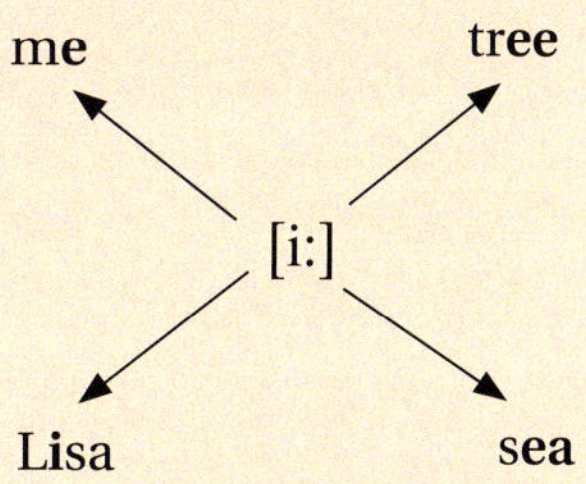

1. Speak to me! Is it a secret?
2. Does he meet Lisa at the beach?
3. It's three metres from the tree to the sea.
4. These football teams eat cheap pizzas on Monday evening.

There are 17 words in these sentences where you say [i:].
Find them and make four lists in your exercise book.

9 Word friends

Which words go together?

1. 'street' and 'party' make 'street party'.
2. 'taxi' … .
   Go on, please.

street	Underground
taxi	Buckingham
Piccadilly	mobile
Hindu	Monday
football	meeting

Palace	Circus
station	place
driver	team
party	phone
evening	temple

10 One word is wrong!

1. temple, palace, church, attic.
   'attic' is wrong.
2. Germany, Europe, England, Italy
   Go on, please.
3. king, father, mother, uncle
4. comic, book, pencil, magazine
5. Underground, taxi, plane, bus
6. late, week, month, year

11 Word puzzles

a) *What's the word?*

1. Kings and queens live in a … .
   – That's a palace.
2. Your father's brother is your … .
   Go on, please.
3. A train leaves and arrives at a … .
4. When people leave one Underground train and go to another, they … .
5. Hindu people don't go to a church, they go to a … .
6. When two people marry there's a … .
7. You can see processions and hear music at a … .

b) *Make more word puzzles for a partner.*

12 A cartoon

London's changed since our last visit!

change – *sich verändern*; since – *seit*

Present simple *(einfache Gegenwart)*

Verwendung:
Du verwendest das present simple*, um über etwas zu sprechen, das regelmäßig oder oft stattfindet.*

I **play** football **every Tuesday**.
He **visits** his grandma **very often**.

Bildung:
- *Verneinung und Fragen werden mit* do *gebildet.*
- He, she, it, *das „s" muss mit!*

I **don't go** to the cinema very often.
How often **do** you **go** to the cinema?
She **goes** to school by bike.
He always **takes** the bus.
It **leaves** in front of his house.

Achtung!
Wenn etwas gerade eben geschieht, wird das present progressive *verwendet.*

I'm sorry, you**'re wearing** the wrong trousers.
But I **wear** these trousers every day!

Welche Beispielsätze passen zu Cartoon A? Warum?

Ought to, must, mustn't

Du verwendest ought to*, um zu sagen, was man eigentlich tun sollte.*

You **ought to** go to work by train, Dad!

Du verwendest must*, um zu sagen, was man tun muss.*

But you **must** buy a ticket.

Du verwendest mustn't*, um zu sagen, was man nicht tun darf.*

You **mustn't** get on the train without a ticket.

Welcher der Beispielsätze passt zu Cartoon B? Warum?

Checklist

Ich kann	
… sagen, wohin ich gerne gehen würde.	I'd like to visit the Notting Hill Carnival.
… sagen, dass ich etwas langweilig finde.	Buckingham Palace is so boring.
… sagen, dass ich etwas toll finde.	The shops in London are awesome.
… sagen, dass etwas regelmäßig geschieht.	He stays with us every summer.
… sagen, dass etwas immer das Gleiche ist.	We always go there.
… sagen, was man eigentlich machen sollte.	We ought to wear Indian clothes.
… sagen, was ich machen muss.	I must leave the house at nine o'clock.
… sagen, was nicht passieren darf.	We mustn't be late.

Checkout: The two camels

One day, a young camel was talking to his father.
"Dad, why do we have humps?" he asked.
"Well, the humps contain fat. That's our food for the many days when we're in the desert."
"Thanks," said the youngster. Then he asked, "Dad, why do we have long eyelashes?"
"Well, son," said the father, "in the desert there are sandstorms with lots of sand. We need long eyelashes to protect our eyes."
"OK. And why do we have such big feet?"
"Well, son, the sand is very soft in the desert. Our big feet stop us sinking into the sand."
"Well thanks, Dad," said the youngster. "So what the heck are we doing in London Zoo?"

Hast du die Geschichte verstanden? Wo leben die Kamele?
Hier gibt es wieder einige Wörter und Wendungen, die du nicht kennst. Du kannst sie aus dem Zusammenhang erschließen oder in der alphabetischen Wortliste ab Seite 107 nachschlagen.

TIPP

Tipps: The two camels

1. was talking: *Das ist die Vergangenheitsform von* is talking.
2. humps, eyelashes: *Diese Körperteile siehst du auf dem Bild.*
3. sandstorm, sinking: *Diese Wörter sind im Deutschen ganz ähnlich.*

It's good to talk!

	Text and talk	Chatterbox
UK phone numbers:		
during the day	30p per minute	20p per minute
evening/weekend	10p per minute	5p per minute
Mobiles in the same network:		
during the day	30p per minute	25p per minute
evening/weekend	10p per minute	5p per minute
Text messages:	15p per message	30p per message
Photo messages:	20p per message	35p per message

Lots of people have got mobile phones, but phone calls aren't always cheap. There are lots of different plans, but phone bills can still be a problem, and some people can't pay them.

1 Phones and plans

a) *Make a list of phone words on these two pages. Add new words to your list as you work through the unit.*

b) *Which plan could be best for you? Say why.*

2 Speaking: On the phone

Act short phone dialogues with a partner. Partner A phones, partner B answers.

Partner A	Partner B
You can ask …	You can say …
where your partner is.	where you are.
can he/she talk?	that you can talk/can't talk because … .
can you meet?	where and when you can meet.
…	…

Remember:
Start and finish the dialogue nicely.
You can also use your own ideas.

Who needs phone boxes?

Say it!

It's me, Linda.	*Ich bin's, Linda.*
Speak to you later.	*Bis dann.*

3 Speaking: Have you got a mobile phone?

a) *Make a survey. Write your partners' answers.*

	Yes	*No*
Have you got a mobile phone?	…	…
Do you always take your mobile phone with you?	…	
Do you sleep with your mobile phone near your bed?	…	
Do you pay your own phone bills?	…	
Do you download ring tones?	…	
Do you send text messages?	…	
Did you get your mobile phone more than a year ago?	…	
…	…	

b) *Talk about your results.*

… people have got a mobile phone. … people always … . *Go on, please.*

b Mobile phone tips

Not everybody wants to listen when you talk on your mobile phone!
Mobile phones can also be dangerous sometimes.
Here are some tips.

1. Switch off your phone in the cinema, a restaurant, the classroom, or the church. Some people are angry when a phone rings in a quiet place.
2. Talk quietly. You don't have to shout. Your friend will hear you.
3. When you have to call somebody, think. Who is sitting behind you? Do they want to hear your problems?
4. Don't use your phone when you're walking along the road, or when you're on a bike or a skateboard! It's dangerous.
5. Be careful with your phone. Somebody could steal it!

Say it!

Talk quietly.	*Sprich leise.*
Switch off your phone in the cinema.	*Schalte dein Handy im Kino aus.*

4 The tips

a) *Which tip goes with which picture?*

1

3

5

2

4

1. Picture number … goes with tip … .
2. *Go on, please.*

b) *Talk about the tips with a partner. Are they good tips for you and your friends?*

Sometimes people ….

That's awful.

I always …. / I never ….

I don't think that's a problem.

5 Speaking: What do you think?

Look what these people are saying. Are they right?

A: Do you think Number 1 is right?
B: No, I don't. I think he's wrong.
A: Why do you think he's wrong?
B: Because …

6 Listening with DJ Dan: In Devon

DJ Dan is talking about mobile phones today. *What's the right answer?*

1. Tim stayed
   a) on a campsite.
   b) in a hotel.
2. One afternoon the boys
   a) went swimming.
   b) walked along the beach.
3. They didn't go back because
   a) they couldn't swim.
   b) it was too dangerous.
4. Tim phoned his parents and
   a) they were angry.
   b) a boat came to get the boys.

7 Writing: A mobile phone story

Did a mobile phone help you or a friend? Or did somebody use a mobile phone and you hated it? *Write about it. Find an ending for the story.*

When did it happen? • Where did it happen?
Who was with you? • What happened?

8 A song: Why didn't you call me?

Gray, Macy/Ruzumna, Jeremy

We went out one night,
Everything went right.
We got something started,
It was outta sight.
We had such a good time,
Hey! Why didn't you call me?

I thought I'd see you again.
By the phone I wait,
Staring into space.
Thinking about our first kiss
Out on our first date.

everything – *alles;* we got something started – *wir haben etwas miteinander angefangen;* outta sight – *toll;* by – *neben;* staring into space – *ins Leere starrend;* kiss – *Kuss;* date – *Verabredung*

Project: Communication

There are many ways to send messages and talk with other people. *Work in groups and do a project about communication. You can do project A or project B.*

A
Look at the history of communication. How did people send messages 100 or 200 years ago?

B
Think about the future of communication. How will people send messages in 50 or 100 years?

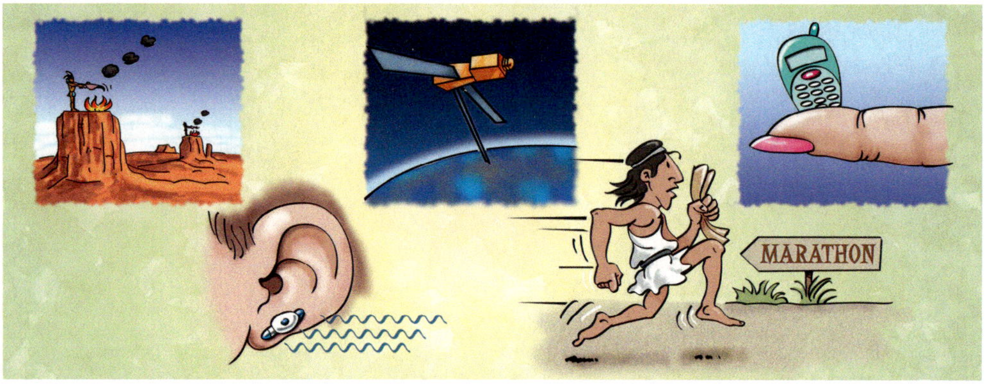

You can show your work to the class in ONE of two ways:

an **exhibition**
with posters and texts

a **presentation**
in English

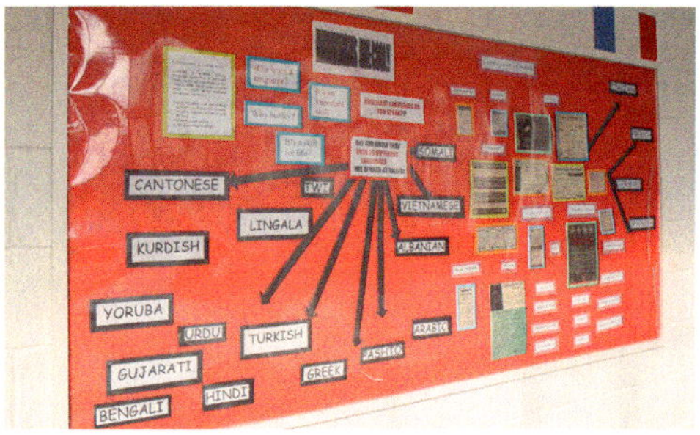

Exhibition
1. Find texts and pictures for your exhibition.
2. Put the pictures and texts into groups. The exhibition should tell a story.
3. Make posters with the pictures and texts. There should be one poster for every part of the story.
4. The pictures shouldn't be too small and the texts must be easy to read. Maybe you can use a computer.
5. What do people in the class think of the exhibition? Make a worksheet for them. Then they can tell you.

Presentation
1. There should be pictures and short texts in your presentation.
2. Put the pictures and short texts into groups. The presentation should tell a story.
3. Make notes on cards. You should say something about every picture and short text.
4. More than one person should do the presentation. That will make it more interesting!
5. Are there any questions at the end of the presentation? Ask the people in the class!

Checklist

Ich kann	
... jemanden fragen, ob er ein Handy besitzt.	Have you got a mobile phone?
... ein Telefongespräch beginnen.	Sarah, is that you? It's me, Linda.
... ein Telefongespräch beenden.	Speak to you later. Bye!
... sagen, dass jemand Recht hat.	I think she's right.
... sagen, dass jemand nicht Recht hat.	I think she's wrong.
... sagen, was jeder haben sollte.	Everybody should have a mobile phone.
... sagen, dass jemand sein Handy ausschalten soll.	Can you switch off your mobile phone, please?

Strategy: Reading

Mobile phones: Who pays the bill?
Soon half of all young people in America will have a mobile phone. Many young people say they can't live without a phone. But mobile phones aren't cheap. Somebody must pay the bills.
Dan Brown is thirteen. Last month his parents got a phone bill for $500. Many young people don't understand their mobile phone plan and it's often more expensive than they think.

Too many mobiles?
Francesca lives in Italy. She is addicted to her mobile phones. She has 9 of them, so she always has reception. She sometimes sends 200 text messages in one day. "When you get lots of messages, your friends think you are really cool," she says.
Lots of teenagers in Italy have Francesca's problem. They are addicted to their mobile phones.

Mit der richtigen Taktik ist Lesen gar nicht so schwer. Erarbeite dir diese zwei Zeitungsausschnitte in drei Schritten.

A Vor dem Lesen
Lies zuerst die Überschrift und überlege:

- *Was könnte alles in dem Text stehen?*
- *Was weiß ich schon über dieses Thema?*
- *Was würde mich noch interessieren?*

So bringst du dein Gehirn in die richtige Stimmung!

B Während des Lesens
Lies den Text nun still für dich. Wichtig dabei ist:

- *Du musst nicht jedes Wort gleich verstehen! Lies erst in Ruhe bis zum Ende.*
- *Frage dich, wie viel du verstanden hast. Alles? Die Hälfte? Gar nichts?*
- *Gehe zurück und lies schwierige Stellen noch einmal. Schreibe dir aus jedem Text 2-3 Wörter heraus, die dir am wichtigsten erscheinen.*

C Nach dem Lesen
Arbeite jetzt mit einem Partner zusammen.

- *Erzählt euch gegenseitig, was in den Texten steht und besprecht Stellen, die ihr nicht verstanden habt.*
- *Erschließt euch unbekannte Wörter aus dem Zusammenhang oder schlagt sie im Wörterbuch nach.*

Wales

a Katja's town is twinned with Abergavenny, a town in Wales. Katja plays the trombone. She's in Abergavenny with a band from her town. She's there on an exchange.

Hallo!
Wir sind in Abergavenny angekommen. Ich wohne bei einer netten Familie.
Sie haben eine Tochter, Kerry.
Wales ist schön! Aber manche Leute hier haben eine total eigene Sprache.
Sie sprechen Walisisch.
Kein Witz! Ich verstehe wirklich kein Wort.
Sie sprechen aber natürlich auch Englisch.

Wales isn't England!

Every boy and girl in Wales must learn the Welsh language at school.

1 A German girl and a Welsh boy

a) *Say in English what Katja writes in her e-mail.*

Katja has arrived in … .
She's staying … . *Go on, please.*

b) *Now tell the class about Rhodri in German.*

Rhodri wohnt in Abergavenny.
Er spricht … . *Go on, please.*

2 Speaking: An exchange visit

A Welsh or English exchange pupil is staying at your house.
Make dialogues with a partner.

put my clothes here? use your computer? watch TV? phone my parents? …

A: This is your room.
B: Great. Can I …?
A: Yes, of course.
B: Can I …?
A: I'm not sure. I'll ask my parents.

There are three million people in Wales – and ten million sheep.

There were lots of coal mines in Wales. Today some are museums.

Numbers in three languages

eins	one	un
zwei	two	dau
drei	three	tri
vier	four	pedwar
fünf	five	pump
sechs	six	chwech
sieben	seven	saith
acht	eight	wyth
neun	nine	naw
zehn	ten	deg

3 Listening: Katja and Kerry

a) Katja is in Kerry's room. They're listening to music. *Right or wrong?*

1. Katja likes the band.
2. Some Welsh bands sing in Welsh.
3. Kerry speaks Welsh like she speaks English.
4. English is older than Welsh.
5. Katja met a boy yesterday evening.
6. Katja doesn't like the boy.

b) *What do you think "Dw i'n dy garu di." means?*

4 More about Wales

Find more information about Wales. Here are some ideas.

What are the biggest towns in Wales?
What other sports do people play in Wales?
What can tourists do there?

b On Monday Rhodri had football training. He was late. The coach was angry.

> **Say it!**
> Where **were** you? — *Wo **warst** du?*
> **Did** you **forget** the training? — ***Hast** du das Training **vergessen**?*

5 What happened?

What's missing?

1. Rhodri … to a concert last night.
2. He … a German girl there.
3. She … the trombone in a band.
4. Rhodri … her again this afternoon.
5. They … to a café.
6. Rhodri … the training.

6 Speaking: Sorry I'm late!

a) *Act the dialogue.*

A: Sorry I'm late!
B: Where were you?
A: I was in town .
B: Did you forget the party ?
A: No, I didn't. I'm sorry!

b) *Make new dialogues with a partner.*

Why were you late?	at the swimming pool	the football game
…	at school	the audition
	at the shops	the meeting
	…	…

c On Wednesday Katja went to the coal mine museum Big Pit. Kerry went with her.

"I don't want to go down the coal mine," said Katja. "Can I stay in the cafeteria?"
"Come on, you'll really like it," said Kerry. "A miner will go with us. My grandad worked here. It was a dangerous job."
"I don't want to go now," said Katja. "I'm waiting for a phone call."
Katja looked at her mobile phone quickly.
"I've got a text message," she said.
She read the message carefully.
It was from Rhodri.

Don't forget the football game on Saturday.
Will you be at the party tonight?

"OK," Katja said happily. "Let's go down the mine now."

Say it!
The job was **dangerous**.
*Die Arbeit war **gefährlich**.*
Katja read the message **carefully**.
*Katja las die Mitteilung **sorgfältig**.*

7 An important message

Match the parts of the sentences.

1. Katja went to a coal mine → on Wednesday.
2. She wanted to stay
3. She looked
4. She was happy
5. "It's from Rhodri,"
6. He wanted to see her at the party

in the evening.
she said happily.
when she read the message.
in the cafeteria.
at her phone quickly.
on Wednesday.

8 Speaking: Let's meet!

You want to do something with a friend at the weekend.

Act dialogues with a partner.

A: Let's go to the school play.
B: I don't want to go there.
A: Come on, you'll really enjoy it.
B: OK. Where do you want to meet?
A: Let's meet outside the library after school.
B: OK. I'll go with you.

Let's go	Let's meet	When?
to the school play	in the cafeteria	at 6 o'clock
to the museum	in the library	on Saturday morning
to Burger Bar	at the station	at 12 o'clock
to Karen's party	at my house	in half an hour
to the leisure centre	in town	after school

Look at pages 26-29 again. What do you know about Katja and Rhodri? Now look at the pictures here. What do you think will happen in the story?

Katja and Rhodri

Rhodri and Katja were in a café. It was Friday afternoon. "I really want to come to the football game tomorrow," said Katja. "You know that. But I can't." "It's OK. It's not a problem," said Rhodri. But he wasn't happy. He liked Katja and he knew that she liked him. Their problem was the next day. Saturday was the German group's last day in Wales. "We're going to visit Carmarthen Castle," said Katja quietly. "Then I must play in a concert in Carmarthen in the evening. It'll be a long day, and the concert is really important." Rhodri didn't say anything.

"I must play in the concert," Katja said again. "This isn't just a holiday. I'm here with the band." "But the football game is important, too," said Rhodri. Then he looked at her. "It's OK. I understand." But Katja wasn't so sure. Did he really understand? 'Maybe he thinks that I don't like him,' she thought. Suddenly she said, "Why don't you come with us? We're a big group. We've got two buses." "I can't," he said. Then he looked at his watch. "Oh, no. I'll be late for training again." He looked at Katja. "Are you sure you can't stay here tomorrow? You can watch our football game. Then we can go into town. What do you think?"

Katja didn't say anything. She needed a good idea now. She wanted to see Rhodri again before she went back to Germany, but she was also part of a band. She really wanted to play in the concert. And she didn't want any problems with the group. "No, I can't," she said. "I'm sorry." "Then I won't see you again?" asked Rhodri. Katja tried to laugh. "Maybe your football team will come to Germany. You can see me then." Rhodri looked at his watch. "I must go. I'm late." He ran quickly out of the café.

When Katja walked home, she suddenly had an idea. In the evening, she talked to Kerry. "I don't feel well," she said. "I can't go on the trip tomorrow." She wasn't happy. But she really wanted to see Rhodri during her last day in Wales.

The next morning Kerry went to Carmarthen, and Katja stayed at home. At ten o'clock she went to the football game. But she didn't see Rhodri. He wasn't in the team.
"I'm looking for Rhodri. Have you seen him?" she asked one of the players after the game.
"He was late again for training yesterday. He isn't in the team."

Katja went to Rhodri's house. Maybe he was ill? "He's gone to Carmarthen," said Rhodri's mother. "He went out at eight o'clock. He didn't eat breakfast. It'll be very late when he comes back. And he forgot his mobile phone."

A week later Katja was in Germany. She got a postcard from Wales. It said:

1 Rhodri and Katja

Five of these sentences are right. Find them.

1. Katja wanted to go to the game.
2. The concert was important.
3. Rhodri didn't go to football training.
4. He went to Carmarthen with Katja.
5. Katja went to the game.
6. Katja was on a different bus.
7. Rhodri sent a postcard to Germany.
8. Katja saw Rhodri at the game.
9. Rhodri wants to see Katja again.

2 Partner towns

Is your town twinned with a town in another country? Try to find out:

- What's the name of the town?
- Where is it?
- What's special about the town?
- …

1 A day in Abergavenny

a) Katja wanted to look at Abergavenny. This is what she did.

walk to the market – interesting

look for a present – buy a cup

go to the museum – closed

visit the castle – look at the dungeon

walk along the river – see some boats

meet Kerry's friends – nice

In the evening Katja told Mrs Baker about the day. *Make sentences.*

1. I walked to the market. It was interesting.
2. Then I looked for … . I bought … .
3. After that I … . *Go on, please.*

b) When Kerry's father came home he had lots of questions about the day in Abergavenny. *Make a dialogue with a partner.*

1. *Mr Baker:* Where did you go today?
   Katja: I … to the market.
2. *Mr Baker:* Did you …?
   Katja: Yes, I did. *Go on, please.*

… go today? | … meet anybody? | … enjoy it? | … visit any nice places? | … buy anything? | … eat anything?

2 Listening: A trip to Big Pit

Big Pit was a coal mine for 1000 [1] years.
Rabbits [2] worked here every day. It's now a museum.
The tour of the mine is three days [3] long.
You will go 900 [4] metres down the mine.
Over 1,000,000 [5] people visit Big Pit every year.
The museum is open from 05:00 – 24:00 [6].

Listen carefully. Find the right words.

Number 1 is '100'.
Number 2 is … . *Go on, please.*

3 An angry coach

Rhodri's coach was angry after the game. *What's right?*

"Where was Luke?" he shouted loud/loudly . "You were very bad/badly . Mark had the ball, and you didn't see him."
"I'm sorry," said Luke quiet/quietly .
The coach looked angry/angrily at his team. "David, you ran too slow/slowly . We should win these games easy/easily. The other team wasn't good/well . Now go to the changing rooms quick/quickly . I don't want to see you again today. We'll talk about it tomorrow."

Say it!

That was **loud**.	*Das war **laut**.*
He shouted **loudly**.	*Er schrie **laut**.*

4 Speaking: How was it?

Act dialogues with a partner. Add your own ideas.

A: I went to a party last night.
B: How was it?
A: It was OK.
B: Did you meet anybody?
A: Yes, I met … ./No, … .

Where?	When?	How was it?
a party	last night	It was OK.
a concert	yesterday	It was cool.
a football game	on Friday	It was awesome.
the leisure centre	at the weekend	It wasn't very good.
…	…	…

5 Mediation: At the Abergavenny football club

Some people in the German group are at the Abergavenny football club. They want to know about the club. One of the Germans doesn't speak English, so Katja must help with the information.

Gegen wen spielt Abergavenny als Nächstes?

Können wir das Spiel hier in Abergavenny anschauen?

Wann ist das nächste Heimspiel? Gegen wen spielt Abergavenny?

Um wie viel Uhr fängt das Spiel an?

Position	Team	Played	Points
1	Monmouth Town	15	39
2	Rogestone	15	39
3	A. C. Pontymiste	16	31
4	Abergavenny	16	27
5	Newtown	13	26

Next away game against
Monmouth Town
Sat 1st January
2 o'clock

Next home game against
Tillery United
Sat 8th January
2 o'clock

TIPP

Arbeiten mit dem Wörterbuch II

Wenn du beim Wörterlernen einmal nicht weißt, wie ein Wort ausgesprochen wird, kannst du in deinem Wörterbuch oder in der alphabetischen Wortliste ab S. 107 ganz einfach die so genannte Lautschrift nachschlagen. Die Lautschrift ist für alle Sprachen gleich und sagt dir genau, wie etwas ausgesprochen wird. Keine Angst, du musst nicht alle Lautschriftzeichen auswendig lernen! Viele sind wie in unserer normalen Schrift. Die anderen Zeichen kannst du jederzeit nachschlagen (S. 91).

Den Umgang mit der Lautschrift kannst du üben. Versuche immer wieder, die Lautschrift im Wörterbuch zu lesen oder auch einmal einzelne Wörter beim Lernen selbst in Lautschrift zu schreiben. Außerdem kannst du die Lautschrift als Geheimsprache verwenden. Kannst du zum Beispiel diesen Text lesen?

he'ləʊ krɪs
haʊ a: ju: kæn wi: mi:t æt sɪks ə'klɒk ɪn frɒnt əv ðə 'swɪmɪŋ pu:l
aɪ wɒnt tʊ tel ju: ə 'si:krət
'li:sə

Lösung: Hello Chris! How are you? Can we meet at six o'clock in front of the swimming pool? I want to tell you a secret. Lisa

6 Word web: Sport and music

Make a word web for 'sport and music' in your exercise book.

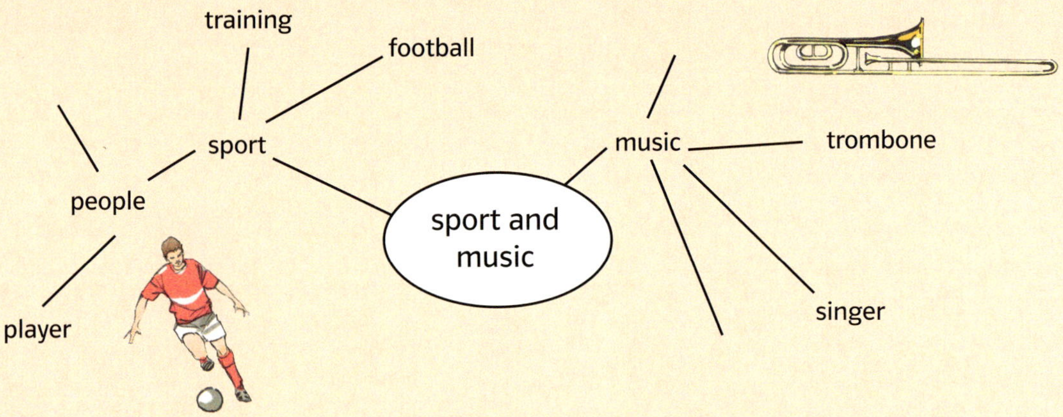

7 Listen and speak

[w]

What's the weather like in Wales?
Very wet, they say.
And it's worse in winter.
Well, we'll take warm anoraks.
And we'll eat hot snacks.

8 Mirror words

Can you read these words?
Use a mirror.

watch	morning	language
forget	tonight	postcard

mirror – Spiegel

9 A cartoon

Some Welsh words are very, very long!

"Two 'N's in 'twinned', Gareth!"

10 Today and yesterday

1
- Let's talk about football. — But we … about that yesterday!

2
- Look at this magazine. — It's boring. I … at it yesterday.

3
- Do you want to watch my DVD? — No, thanks. I … it … .

4
- Don't forget your training today. — I know. I … it … .

5
- Can you hear that noise? — Yes, I can. I … it …, too.

6
- Don't sit there! — Why not? I … .

Write the answers.

1. But we talked about that yesterday!
2. *Go on, please.*

11 What's my job?

1

2

3

4

5

6

1. Number 1 is a DJ.
2. Number 2 is … . *Go on, please.*

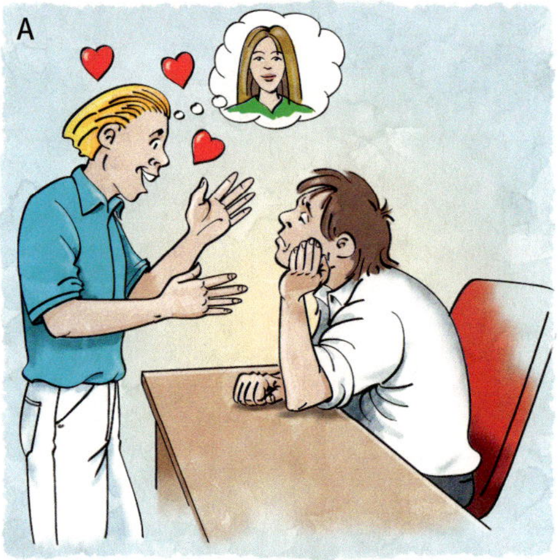

Past simple *(Vergangenheit)*

Verwendung:
Du verwendest das past simple*, um über Dinge zu sprechen, die in der Vergangenheit passiert sind.*

Bildung:
Meist wird -ed *an das Verb angehängt.*
Es gibt auch unregelmäßige Formen.
Die Formen von be *sind* was *und* were.

Achtung!
Verneinung und Fragen werden mit did *und der Grundform des Verbs gebildet. Es wird kein* -ed *mehr an das Verb angehängt!*

I **went** to a concert last night.
I **met** a German girl there.
She **played** in a band.

He **looked** into his wallet.
Then he **bought** the new computer game.
Where **were** you? – I **was** at home.

I **didn't see** her yesterday.
Did she **stay** at home?

Welche Beispielsätze passen zu Cartoon A? Warum?

Adjectives and adverbs *(Adjektive und Adverbien)*

Verwendung:
Adjektive beschreiben Personen, Ereignisse und Sachen.
Adverbien beschreiben, wie etwas geschieht.

Bildung:
- *Die meisten Adjektive werden durch Anhängen von* -ly *zu Adverbien.*
- *Es gibt aber auch unregelmäßige Formen.*

Achtung!
Im Deutschen gibt es diese Unterscheidung nicht!

The job is very **dangerous**.

But he always works **carefully**.

The trombone is a **nice** instrument.
But only if you play it **nicely**!
It was a very **good** game.
You played **well**.

Das Spiel war **gut**.
Ihr habt **gut** gespielt.

Welche Beispielsätze passen zu Cartoon B? Warum?

Checklist

Ich kann	
… über Wales sprechen.	They speak Welsh in Wales.
… fragen, wo jemand war.	Where were you?
… sagen, was ich gestern gemacht habe.	I went to a football game.
… sagen, wie etwas war.	The concert was great!
… fragen, ob jemand etwas vergessen hat.	Did you forget the training?
… beschreiben, wie etwas ist.	This picture is very nice.
… beschreiben, wie etwas geschieht.	She laughed happily.
… sagen, dass jemand etwas gut kann.	He sings very well.

Checkout: Two tricks

The hole in the hand
Take a sheet of paper and roll it up. Hold the rolled up sheet of paper close to your left eye. Look with both your eyes at something about five metres away. Then put your other hand in front of your right eye. There's now a hole in your hand.

The third finger
Put the tips of your index fingers together at eye level in front of your face. Focus on a white wall two or three metres behind your fingers. Pull them apart slowly. You can now see another finger in the middle.

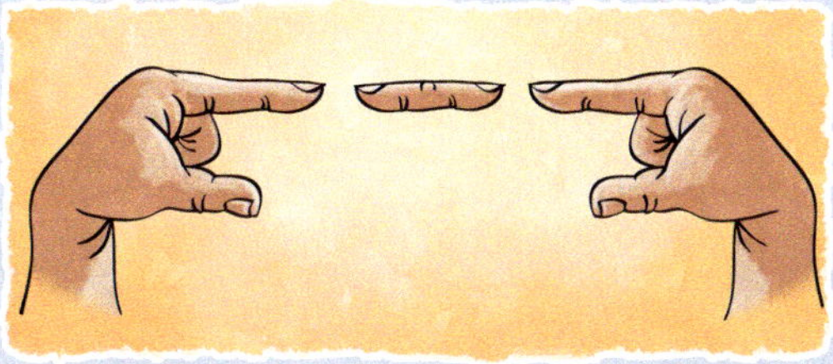

Haben die beiden Tricks bei dir funktioniert?
Hier gibt es wie immer einige Wörter und Wendungen, die du nicht kennst. Du kannst sie aus dem Zusammenhang erschließen oder in der alphabetischen Wortliste ab Seite 107 nachschlagen.

TIPP

Tipps: Two tricks
1. rolled up sheet of paper, hole, index finger: *Diese Dinge siehst du alle in der Zeichnung.*
2. *Habe Geduld und lies den Text mehrere Male durch. Nicht bei jedem funktionieren optische Täuschungen gleich.*

Is school cool?

a You already know lots of things about British schools.
Work in groups and find words for:
school subjects: Maths, …
school people: caretaker, …
school rooms: cafeteria, …

My name is Alexandra Young. I go to Westlands High School. There are over a thousand pupils at my school. We all wear the Westlands uniform, but I don't like it. I hate black shoes.

My school day starts at eight thirty. First we have morning registration. The teacher checks that we are all there. Then we have our lessons. The lunch break is at 12.30. I always eat in the school cafeteria. My favourite meal is fish and chips.

Grades in Britain:	Grades in Germany:
A	1
B	2
C	3
D	4
E	5/6

We have homework every day. I usually do it in the evening. There are lots of tests, too. I got a B in my last English test. I was happy with that grade.

1 Alexandra's school

What's wrong?

1. Westlands School has got 800 pupils. That's wrong. It's got … .
2. The school day starts at nine o'clock.
3. She never eats in the school cafeteria.
4. Alexandra does her homework in the evening.
5. She got an A in her English test.
6. She hasn't enjoyed History this year.
7. Her project was awful.
8. The art club meets in the lunch break.

2 Two schools

Make notes about the two schools.

Westlands	**My school**
a uniform	no uniform
…	…

uniform cafeteria
day starts at … reports
number of pupils grades …

Westlands High School

Subject profile: History

Name: *Alexandra Young*
Tutor group: *9GP*
Teacher: *Mr Barnes*

PUPIL
Last year I wasn't really interested in History. This year I've really enjoyed the subject. It's interesting with Mr Barnes. I've tried to work harder this year. I think my work is quite good.

TEACHER
Alexandra has worked hard this term. She has got some good ideas, and she is very interested in History. She always does her homework. Her project about Britain in 1950 was very good.

This is my profile for History. Every year we get a profile for all our subjects. We must write a report and say how good or bad we think we are. Then the teachers write how good or bad we really are.

I'm in the art club. We draw pictures and make things. The club meets every Wednesday after school. My best friend is in the club, too. It's fun!

Sports hall

3 Speaking: A visit

An English pupil is visiting your school. *Act the dialogue with a partner.*

A: How big is your school?
B: It's got … pupils, I think.
A: When does the school day start?
B: It starts at … . *Go on, please.*

Where do you …? Are there lots of …?
Do you have …? …

4 A profile

a) *Write a profile for one of your subjects. Say how good or bad you are.*

b) *Read your friend's profile. Is it true?*

I'm quite good at … now.
I think … better this year.
I've worked … .
…

b

School information

School rules
- You must stay at school during the school day.
- Do not eat and drink in classrooms.
- Always wear a school uniform when you are at school. Pupils may not wear earrings at school.
- Do not use mobile phones during lessons.
- Do not bully other pupils.

Bullying
When pupils bully other pupils, they:
- push or kick them every day.
- say awful things to them every day.
- send them lots of awful text messages.

Westlands School says **NO** to bullying!

School sanctions
Here are some of the school's sanctions:
- Detention (pupils must come after school or on Saturday)
- Letter or phone call to parents
- Pupils must leave the school.
- Parents must come to school and talk to the headteacher.
- Pupils must stay at home for one day.
- Extra homework

5 Rules and sanctions

a) *What must pupils do? What mustn't they do? Make two lists.*

must	mustn't
stay at school	eat and drink in classrooms
…	…

b) *Talk about the sanctions with a partner.*

A: A detention on Saturday is terrible.
B: I'm not sure. I think it's worse when your parents … . *Go on, please.*

c) *What rules and sanctions are there at your school? Make two lists. Is your school stricter than Westlands School?*

6 Listening with DJ Dan: Four pupils

Today Dan is talking about school rules and what happens when you break them. He's talking to four young people.
Two of these sanctions are not in the text. Which are they?

1. You must give money to the school.
2. A pupil must leave the school.
3. You must go to school with your parents.
4. You get a detention in the lunch break.
5. You get a Saturday detention.
6. You must do extra homework.

7 Writing: What happened?

Write about a situation when you or a friend broke a school rule. Say what happened.

I / My friend ran / wore / talked / … .
I / He / She … .
Then … .
…

The teacher saw / heard / … .
He / She gave … .
I / We had to … .
My / Our parents … .

8 On the wall

Which is the best message?

knock – *klopfen*; no sleep at all – *überhaupt kein Schlaf*; keep your mouth shut – *den Mund halten*; bite – *beißen*; if – *wenn*

Project: Bullying

Bullying is a problem in lots of schools.

One girl's story
Some pupils are bullying me at school. I tried to talk to them, but it hasn't stopped. They make jokes about the style of my hair. They say I'm a freak. I don't think it will get better.
Naomi, 14

Is somebody bullying you?
We can help you!
Childline
0800 11 11
www.childline.org.uk

Work in groups and do a project about bullying. You can show your work to the class in ONE of two different ways.

a short play in English

a poster with rules for your class

Say **NO**
to bullying!

These are our rules
for Class 7d:

Organize your work:

1. Plan it!
   Decide: a play or a poster? Who does which job? Where do you start?
2. Do it!
   Find information and write the texts.
   Play: Think about what you need for the play. Practise the dialogues.
   Poster: Think about a design for your poster and find or draw pictures.
3. Present it!
   Show your poster to the class or act the play for them.
4. Talk about it!
   What was good and what was bad? How can you make it better next time?

Checklist

Ich kann	
…über meine Schule sprechen.	There are over a thousand pupils at my school.
…über meinen Schultag sprechen.	My school day starts at eight thirty.
…über meine Fächer sprechen.	I'm quite good at German.
…über meine Noten sprechen.	I got a B in my last English test.
…über Regeln in der Schule sprechen.	You mustn't use mobile phones at school.
…über Schulstrafen sprechen.	A girl in my class got detentions.
…über Probleme in der Schule sprechen.	Bullying is a problem in our school.

Strategy: Writing

Eine kleine Geschichte auf Englisch zu schreiben ist gar nicht so schwer! Hier sind einige Tipps, wie du vorgehen kannst.

A *Vor dem Schreiben*

- *Du entscheidest dich für ein persönliches Erlebnis, über das du schreiben möchtest, z.B. eine lustige Geschichte aus dem Urlaub, ein Erlebnis in der Schule oder etwas über dein Haustier.*
- *Du schreibst die Fragewörter* who, what, when, where, why, what then *auf ein Blatt Papier. Notiere dir hinter jedem Wort einige Stichpunkte, z. B.*

  Who? – my dog Max
  What? – ran after the cat

B *Während des Schreibens*

- *Überlege dir die ersten Sätze, z. B.:*
  Last week on Thursday my dog Max ran after our cat. The cat climbed on a tree and Max … .
- *Schreibe dann die ganze Geschichte auf. Du kannst dich dabei an deinen Notizen zu den Fragewörtern orientieren. Wörter, die du nicht weißt, kannst du auf Deutsch aufschreiben und später im Wörterbuch nachschlagen, z. B.*
  They needed a big long *Leiter* to get him out of the tree.

C *Nach dem Schreiben*

- *Lies die ganze Geschichte durch. Nimm dir Stellen, die sich ‚komisch' anhören, noch einmal vor.*
- *Gib die Geschichte einem Partner zum Lesen. Verbessere die Fehler, die er gefunden hat.*
- *Überlege dir eine gute Überschrift für deine Geschichte, z. B: Max's accident.*
- *Gib die Geschichte deiner Lehrerin oder deinem Lehrer zur Korrektur.*
- *Schreibe zum Schluss eine ‚saubere' Version deiner Geschichte. Wenn du möchtest, kannst du sie mit Bildern oder Zeichnungen gestalten.*

Grammar

1 Questions and answers

Find the right answers.

1. What would you like to do in London?	No, I haven't. My old one is OK.
2. Have you got any ideas for tomorrow?	You can take the Underground.
3. Can I wear my old T-shirt and jeans?	Let's meet in the new café. It's cool!
4. How can I go to the Science Museum?	I'd like to visit the West End.
5. Have you got a new mobile phone?	No, you ought to wear nice clothes.
6. Can I use your mum's computer?	I went shopping and forgot to call you.
7. Why were you late yesterday?	I could show you the London Eye.
8. Where can we meet after school?	I'm not sure. I'll ask my mum first.

2 Good tips

What's missing?

must (2x) mustn't (3x) ought to (3x)

1. This was the last time! You … be late for training again.
2. You … help your friend with his Maths homework. He helped you with German.
3. You … use your mobile phone during lessons.
4. You … stay at school during the school day.
5. He … do more sport, but he's very lazy.
6. You … do this diet every day or it won't help.
7. You … bully other pupils. That's awful!
8. She … write this again, but I don't think there is enough time.

3 Speaking: Did you forget …?

Make dialogues with a partner.

You	Your partner
Frage, ob er/sie euer Treffen gestern vergessen hat.	Sage ja. Entschuldige dich.
Frage, wo er/sie war.	Sage, dass du auf dem Markt warst.
Frage, ob es ihm gefallen hat und ob er etwas gekauft hat.	Sage, dass es sehr cool war. Du hast ein schönes Geschenk für einen Freund/eine Freundin gekauft.
Sei empört. Sage, dass du ihn/sie nicht mehr sehen möchtest.	Sage, dass es dir Leid tut. Schlage vor, morgen darüber zu reden.
Verabschiede dich.	Verabschiede dich.

Words

4 The wrong word

a) *Find the wrong word.*

1. caretaker – headmaster – teacher – driver – pupils
2. English – Welsh – France – German – Chinese
3. do it – listen to it – talk about it – plan it – present it
4. awful – great – awesome – fantastic – cool
5. concert – sing – message – audition – dance
6. plan – bill – topic – network – ring tone

b) *Make an English-German list of the words.*

caretaker – Hausmeister
headmaster –

5 How can you do it?

a) *How can you speak? Make a word web.*

1.

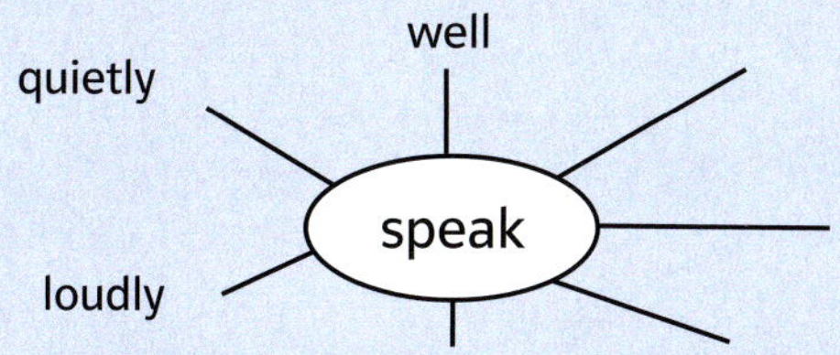

well	badly
quickly	slowly
loudly	quietly
angrily	crazily
happily	…

b) *How can you run, dance, …? Make word webs for these words.*

1. run
2. dance
3. shout
4. draw
5. eat
6. sing
7. play the guitar
8. play football

6 Topics

Write a short text about one of these topics. Tell your class about it.

Wales
language
towns
museums
sports
how many people
…

My mobile phone
cheap
expensive
old
modern
I can …
I use it for …

London
interesting sights
museums
palaces
festivals
Underground
…

Scotland

What you can do in Scotland

a Scotland has got lots of mountains and large lakes. It's very nice in summer, but it often rains. In winter it can be very cold. Many people come to Scotland to enjoy nature.

There are lots of activities in the mountains. Climb Ben Nevis! It's the highest mountain in Scotland.

Not many people live in Scotland.
Germany: about 82 million
England: about 50 million
Scotland: about 5 million

Look for Nessie the Monster! People say she lives in Loch Ness. 'Loch' is the Scottish word for a lake.

Ride a bike along a bike route or sit on a beach.

Many people visit the city of Edinburgh. They look at the famous castle, or they go to the Edinburgh Festival.

Where you can stay in Scotland

The Ness House B&B

5 bedrooms
£25-£32 per person per night

Lots of tourists stay in a 'bed and breakfast'. These are rooms in a small private house.

Oban Hostel

£13.50 per night in July and August
Children £11.75

Scotland's youth hostels are often in the most beautiful places. You have to sleep in a room with other people. There's usually a kitchen and a games room, too.

Jenny's Cottage

Two bedrooms, bathroom, living room with TV, kitchen.
£475 per week (July/August)
Sorry, no pets!

Some families like to stay in a cottage. They can cook their own meals.

1 The right information

a) *These sentences are wrong. What's the right information?*

1. Lots of people live in Scotland.
2. There are no mountains and lakes.
3. The weather is nice in winter, but it often rains.
4. People think a monster lives on Ben Nevis.
5. There is a famous lake in Edinburgh.
6. Nessie is the name of a lake.

b) *Where would you like to stay? Say why.*

2 Speaking: A holiday in Scotland?

a) Your partner wants to go to Scotland. *Act the dialogue.*

A: When do you want to go to Scotland?
B: In July, maybe for one week.
A: What would you like to do?
B: I'd like to ride along a bike route.
A: Where are you going to stay?
B: In a youth hostel.
A: I hope you have a good time.

b) *Make new dialogues.*

May, 10 days? August, 2 weeks …	climb Ben Nevis look for Nessie …

cottage youth hostel B&B …

3 Listening: Two holidays

Simon and Gemma are talking about their holidays in Scotland.
Listen and take notes.

1. Did Simon enjoy his holiday? *Say why or why not.*
2. Did Gemma enjoy her holiday? *Say why or why not.*

b Andrew McWilliams lives in Scotland. His parents work at the Ness House. Andrew often helps his parents.

Today Andrew is in the kitchen. His parents are making breakfast for their guests. Mr McWilliams has just been in the dining room.
"Mrs Schmidt has just come down," he says. "She's ordered a vegetarian breakfast."
"I've already made one," says Mrs McWilliams. "Can you take it to her, Andrew?"
"Mr and Mrs Uddin have asked for orange juice," says Mr McWilliams. "And their daughter has just broken a cup."
"Andrew, go and tidy up, please. Oh, you haven't taken the toast to Mrs Schmidt yet," says Mrs McWilliams.
"And you haven't carried Mrs Spencer's bags to her car," shouts Mr McWilliams. "You haven't done anything yet."
"Just a minute, please. I can't do everything, Dad," says Andrew. "I'm not Superman."

Say it!

She**'s ordered** a vegetarian breakfast.	*Sie **hat** ein vegetarisches Frühstück **bestellt**.*
You **haven't taken** the toast to Mrs Schmidt yet.	*Du **hast** Frau Schmidt den Toast noch **nicht gebracht**.*

4 So much stress!

1. Mr McWilliams has just been in the dining room.
2. Mrs Schmidt … . *Go on, please.*
3. The Uddins … .
4. Their daughter … .
5. Andrew hasn't … .
6. And he hasn't … .

… a vegetarian breakfast
… orange juice
… Mrs Spencer's bags …
… a cup
… the dining room …
… the toast …

5 Speaking: I haven't done it yet!

a) *Write two sentences. Write what you've done this week and what you haven't done. Write your name.*

b) *Give your card to your partner. Your partner must tell the class what you've done and what you haven't done.*

I've finished my Geography project. I haven't done my Maths homework yet. Max

I've visited my uncle and my cousins this week. I haven't visited any friends. Andrea

Max has finished his Geography project. He hasn't done his Maths homework yet.

c The people in the Ness House often ask Andrew questions.

Say it!

Have you **booked** our boat trip yet?	***Hast*** *du unsere Bootsfahrt schon* ***gebucht****?*
Have you **ever been** to Germany?	***Warst*** *du* ***schon einmal*** *in Deutschland?*

6 Has he or hasn't he?

Match the parts of the sentences.

1. Andrew hasn't →	been in the garden.
2. The girl has	seen Nessie.
3. The dog hasn't	already eaten the dog.
4. Maybe Nessie has	seen strange things on the lake.
5. Andrew has never	lost her dog.
6. But people have	→ booked the boat trip yet.

7 Speaking: Have you ever ... ?

Ask your partner.

1. *A:* Have you ever seen a photo of Nessie?
   B: No, I haven't. Not yet!
2. *A:* … . *Go on, please.*

seen a photo of Nessie?
lost/found a pet?
stayed in a hotel?
helped in a shop or hotel?
been to Berlin?
visited a famous castle?

Yes, I have.
No, I haven't.
Not yet!

A photo of Nessie?

One day in August a family arrived at the Ness House for their summer holiday. They had a son, Tom, and a daughter, Helen. Tom was 13, like Andrew.
"Your son can play football with our son, Andrew," said Mr McWilliams.

The next day Tom met Andrew and they played football in the garden. Later they sat down and talked.
"Does Nessie really live in Loch Ness?" asked Tom. "And have you seen her?"
Andrew laughed. "Everybody asks me this," he said. "I don't go to the lake very often. I have sometimes seen something in the lake. But when it's dark, you can't be sure."
"Where's the best place to look?" Tom asked.
"I know a good place," said Andrew. "Some people have seen something there. You should go before it's dark. You can go there this evening. But I can't come with you. I want to visit a friend."
"OK. But why should I go so late?"
"I think Nessie comes up to breathe before it gets dark," answered Andrew.
Tom laughed.
"Let's go," said Andrew. "I'll show you where the place is."

Andrew and Tom walked out of the garden. They took a path to the lake. Andrew found a place near some bushes.
"This is the place," said Andrew. "I'm not sure you'll see anything, but take a camera. You could be lucky."
"OK, I'll come back later with a camera."
The two boys walked back to the house.
"Sorry, I can't come with you," said Andrew, "but I'll be at my friend's house."

In the evening Tom's sister wanted to come with him. Tom and Helen took the same path before it was dark. They sat down and waited. Tom had his camera. It was very quiet on the lake. They couldn't hear anything. It was almost dark, so they couldn't see much on the water. Tom looked at his watch.

Suddenly they heard a noise. "What was that?" asked Helen. Tom got up and looked over the water. "I don't know," he said after a minute. They could see something on the dark water. "Look," said Helen. "Is that Nessie's head?" Something went slowly through the water and made a strange noise. "Andrew was right." Tom was sure now. "She comes up in the evening to breathe." "Take a photo quickly, maybe we can sell it," said Helen. Tom took the photo. But then he was worried. "I think Nessie has seen us. She's swimming to us." Tom and Helen ran back along the path to the Ness House.

Behind the bushes Andrew and his friend tried not to laugh. Andrew's friend took his model of a boat with Nessie's head out of the water. Andrew put the remote control in a bag. They walked back to his friend's house. When they were in the house, they started to laugh loudly. Andrew and his friend loved these jokes. They were the best thing about Loch Ness.

Back in the lake, something swam quietly through the dark water …

1 Three texts

Two of the texts have got wrong information in them. Which text is right?

1. Tom played football with Andrew. Then the two boys went to the lake. They saw something in the water. Tom took a photo of Nessie, but Helen played a trick on them.
2. Tom and his sister were in the Ness House with their parents. One day they took a photo of Nessie. But Tom knew that Nessie was a model of a boat.
3. One evening Tom and his sister went to Loch Ness. They saw something in the water and Tom took a photo. They were scared. They didn't know it was a trick.

2 Andrew's story

Andrew wants to tell his friends about the trick. *Tell his story.*

This is so funny. A boy and a girl are staying at the Ness House. I played football with … . He asked me about … . I took him … . In the evening my friend and I … .

1 Activities in Scotland

What have these people just done?

1. They've just climbed a mountain.
2. She's … .
   Go on, please.

climb a mountain	visit a museum
see Nessie	take a photo of the castle
ride along a bike route	swim in the sea

2 So busy!

What has Andrew done?
What hasn't he done? Make sentences.

1. Andrew has booked a boat trip for Mrs Schmidt.
2. He hasn't … .
   Go on, please.

Andrew
book a boat trip for Mrs Schmidt ✓
tidy up the kitchen ✗
check the e-mail ✓
look for the girl's dog ✗
take the new TV to room 7 ✓
…

3 Listening: Tammy the marathon swimmer

What's the right answer?

1. Tammy is from …
   a) Scotland,
   b) Australia,
   c) England.

2. Tammy swam for …
   a) 6 hours and 9 minutes,
   b) 9 hours and 6 minutes,
   c) 3 hours and 9 minutes.

3. Loch Ness is …
   a) very cold,
   b) not so cold,
   c) like a swimming pool.

4. When Tammy swims, she remembers …
   a) jokes,
   b) music,
   c) Maths problems.

4 Speaking: Lucy and Sarah

Lucy is in a youth hostel with her friend Sarah.

Act the dialogue with a partner.

Lucy: We must leave early tomorrow.
Have you checked the bus times yet?
Sarah: Yes, I have. I checked them last night.
Lucy: Have you phoned your parents yet?
Sarah: Yes, I have. I … them at six o'clock.
Go on, please.

Check the bus times?	… last night.
Answer your e-mails?	… this morning.
Buy a present for your mum?	… on Monday.
Phone your parents?	… at six o'clock.
Send a postcard?	… yesterday.
Pack all your clothes?	… an hour ago.

5 Speaking: At the information centre

Jenny works at the information centre. Some young people would like to visit different places.
Make dialogues with a partner.

Have you visited a castle?

→ Yes, we have. → What did you think of it? → It was cool/awesome/boring/…

→ No, we haven't. → Well, you should. You'll enjoy it. → Thanks for the tip. We'll do that.

1. visit a castle

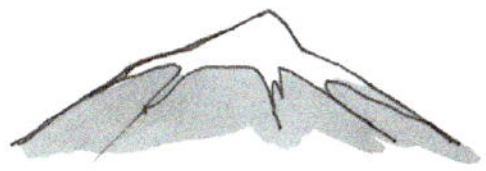

2. climb Ben Nevis

3. ride along bike route

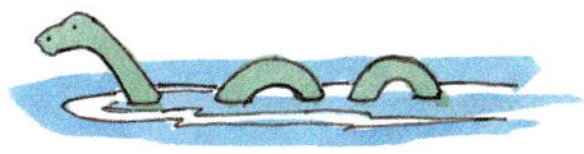

4. see the Loch Ness Monster Exhibition

6 Mediation: In a youth hostel

You're in a youth hostel. A German girl, Gina, has problems with English.
Help her to talk to the man from the youth hostel.

Gina: Ich habe drei Tage gebucht, aber ich würde gerne eine Woche in der Jugendherberge bleiben.
You: My friend has booked … .
Man: She can only stay five days. After that a group from Italy will come here.
You: …
Gina: Kannst du ihn fragen, ob es andere Jugendherbergen in der Nähe gibt?
You: …
Man: Yes, there's a nice youth hostel near here. I can phone for her.
You: …
Gina: Danke, das ist sehr nett von ihm.
You: …

TIPP

Arbeiten mit dem Wörterbuch III

Ein Wort, das du nicht kennst, kannst du im Wörterbuch nachschlagen. Aber aufgepasst, ein Wort kann trotzdem ganz verschiedene Bedeutung haben! Nimm zum Beispiel diesen Satz:

It was a very hot day.
But we had a big fan in our room,
so it was nice and cool.

Von was ist hier die Rede? Schlage das Wort *fan* in einem Wörterbuch nach. Du wirst sehen, dass es zwei sehr unterschiedliche Dinge bedeuten kann. Was passt in diesem Zusammenhang?

Hier sind noch einige weitere Beispiele. Die unterstrichenen Wörter kennst du eigentlich schon. Aber passt die bisherige Bedeutung hier? Schlage die Wörter nach und überlege was richtig ist.

1. The best team will win a cup.
2. I looked down into the well but I couldn't see any water.
3. Don't park the car here. You'll get a ticket!

7 Word web: Nature

Make a word web for 'nature' in your exercise book.

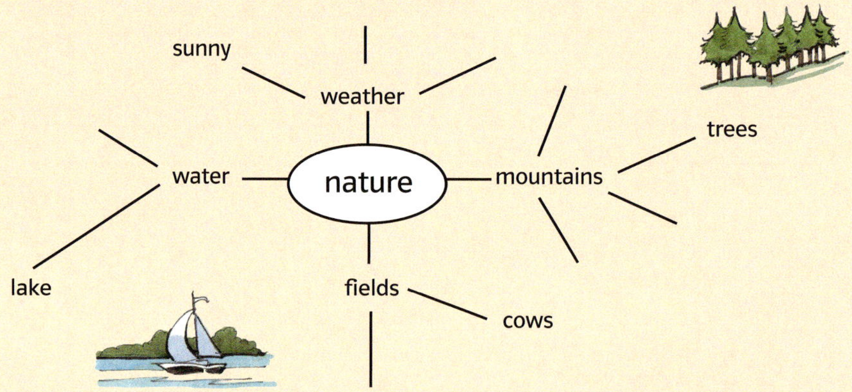

8 Match the words

1. 'Mountain' goes with 'climb'.
   You can climb a mountain.
2. 'Bike' goes with … .
   Go on, please.

mountain • bike	stay • swim
lake • hotel	climb • drive
meal • air	order • ride
trip • car	breathe • book

9 Listen and speak: Same sound, different spelling

a) *One word hasn't got a long [u:] sound. Find it.*

1. argue you make pupil
2. museum town food shoe
3. green fruit blue uniform
4. Tuesday new knew leave
5. room group knife spoon

[u:]
- **u** museum …
- **ou** you
- **ue** blue …
- **ui** …
- **oe** …
- **ew** …

b) *Put the words in different groups.*

10 The Edinburgh Festival

What's missing?

at • in • to • from • by

When is it?
The Edinburgh Festival takes place every year … summer. People come … the festival … many different countries.

What can I do?
You can listen … music and you can go … lots of different events. There are more than 100 different events.

How can I get there and where can I stay?
You can go … Edinburgh … train or you can take a flight there. Many people stay … hotels. But you can also go … a bed and breakfast. Other people stay … a campsite. They go … bus … the events. You can buy some tickets … the tourist information centre.

11 Do you know?

What do people in Scotland call six rainy weeks?

summer

Present perfect *(Perfekt)*

Verwendung:
Du verwendest das present perfect,

- *um zu sagen, was gerade eben passiert ist,*

  She **has** just **broken** a cup.
  They**'ve ordered** an English breakfast.

- *um zu sagen, was bereits erledigt ist,*

  I**'ve** already **made** their breakfast.
  But I **haven't tidied up** their room yet.

- *um darüber zu sprechen, was du schon einmal erlebt oder getan hast.*

  Have you ever **seen** Nessie?
  No, I **haven't**. But I**'ve seen** a ghost!

Bildung:
Das present perfect *wird mit einer Form von* have *und der dritten Verbform gebildet.*

I **have washed** my trousers.
She **has taken** lots of photos.

Achtung!
Hier gibt es viele unregelmäßige Formen (siehe Tabelle S. 132)!

take – took – **taken**
see – saw – **seen**
read – read – **read** (*Aussprache!*)

Achtung Zeitvergleich!
Das present perfect *wird verwendet, um auszudrücken, ob man etwas überhaupt getan hat.*

Have you **done** your homework?
Yes, I **have**. Here it is!

Das past simple *wird verwendet, um zu sagen, dass man etwas zu einem bestimmten Zeitpunkt getan und abgeschlossen hat.*

When **did** you **do** your homework?
I **did** it yesterday evening.

Welche Beispielsätze passen zu den beiden Cartoons? Warum?

Checklist

Ich kann	
… sagen, was ich schon erledigt habe.	I've washed it already.
… sagen, was ich noch nicht erledigt habe.	I haven't tidied up my room yet.
… fragen, ob jemand etwas schon erledigt hat.	Have you done your homework yet?
… fragen, ob jemand etwas schon einmal gemacht hat.	Have you ever played cricket?
… fragen, wo jemand schon einmal gewesen ist.	Have you ever been to Scotland?
… sagen, dass ich etwas noch nie getan habe.	I've never stayed in a hotel.
… jemandem Fragen zu seinem Urlaub stellen.	When do you want to go to Scotland?

Checkout: A bad idea!

A man called Fred Wilder entered a doughnut shop in a small village in Arkansas. He put a pillowcase over his head and shouted at the man behind the counter to give him all the money. Then Wilder realized that something wasn't right – he had forgotten to cut eyeholes in his pillowcase!
So he raised it a bit to see what he was doing. One of the other people in the shop recognized Wilder when he did this and later told the police his name. The police soon found him and sent him to prison. His story was in all the newspapers and the whole nation laughed at him – what a dummy!

Ein Überfall ist immer eine schlechte Idee. Hast du verstanden, an was Fred Wilder außerdem nicht gedacht hat? Hier gibt es wieder einige Wörter und Wendungen, die du nicht kennst. Du kannst sie aus dem Zusammenhang erschließen oder in der alphabetischen Wortliste ab Seite 107 nachschlagen.

TIPP

Tipps: A bad idea!
1. had forgotten: *Diese Vergangenheitsform von* forget *ist so ähnlich wie im Deutschen.*
2. was doing: *Das ist die Vergangenheitsform von* is doing.
3. pillowcase, counter, doughnut: *Diese Dinge sind alle auf dem Bild zu sehen.*

My music

a

I sing in a heavy metal band with my friends. We practise every week. Music is very important for me, but I don't like jazz or classical music. I've got a CD player and a radio in my room. I also download music from the internet, and I've got an MP3 player that can play 20,000 songs.

I totally love Javine. I think she's got a great voice. She's my favourite pop star. I listen to 'Missing you' every day. I always play it loudly. I've just broken up with my boyfriend, so it really helps. You can't see my bedroom walls. I've got so many posters of her. She's the best!

1 Who's who?

1. … played an instrument but didn't enjoy the lessons.
   – That's Justin.
2. … has got lots of posters of a singer.
   – That's … . *Go on, please.*
3. … is a singer in a band. Music is very important for him/her.
4. … listens to the same song every day.
5. … downloads music.
6. … sometimes listens to the radio, but isn't so interested in music.

2 Music words

Make groups with the words on these pages. You can add your own words.

Music styles: heavy metal, …
Instruments: recorder, …
Groups: band, …
How you can listen to music: radio, …

I had recorder lessons at my old school. The teacher was very strict, and her lessons were so boring. My cousin plays the trumpet in her school orchestra. That's a much better instrument. I sometimes listen to music on the radio, but I'm not so interested in it.

A questionnaire about music

1. Who's your favourite band or singer?
2. Why do you like him / her / them?
3. What's your favourite song?
4. Is there a song that reminds you of a person or special event?
5. Do you and your friends like the same music?
6. When do you listen to music?
7. Are your parents angry when you play music loudly?
8. Do you listen to the radio?
9. Do you buy CDs or do you download music from the internet?
10. Do you play an instrument? (What?)
11. No? Would you like to play an instrument?
12. What instrument would you like to play?
13. Can you read music?

Say it!

Music is very important for me.
Musik ist sehr wichtig für mich.
I totally love Javine.
Ich mag Javine sehr.

3 Speaking: Your music

a) *Work with a partner. One of you asks the questions from the questionnaire. The other answers them.*

A: Who's your favourite band or singer?
B: I totally love … .
A: Why do you like them / him / her?
B: He's got a great voice.
A: Go on, please.

b) *Tell the class about six of your partner's answers.*

Christof's favourite band is … .
His favourite song is … .
He often listens to music … .
Go on, please.

b Tell us what you think about your favourite singer or band! Why do you like them? Are you angry or unhappy with them? Then write to us. The best letters and e-mails will win a cool prize.

You can also text us.

McFly: Why can't all boys be so good-looking?

I totally love McFly. They're so cool. Why aren't the boys in my school so good-looking?
Kelly, Cardiff

I couldn't believe it when Matrix split. I'm so upset. My friends and I wore black for one week.
Jade, London

I like Katie Young's music. I really like the lyrics. She sings about problems that I have. She really understands me and my problems.
Emma, Birmingham

Say it!
I like the clothes **that** they wear.
*Ich mag die Kleidung, **die** sie tragen.*

Yellow are an awesome band. They're the best. I like the clothes that they wear.
Ben, London

I was shocked to see a photo of Mark from Yellow with his girlfriend. In every interview he always says he doesn't have a girlfriend. Pop stars have to say things like that, so that they'll be more popular with girls and sell more CDs. That makes me really angry!
Tara, London

I really hate Katie Young. I think her last CD was awful. I don't have one friend that has bought it. I don't know why people listen to her.
Luke, Bristol

4 Titles and texts

Match these titles with the texts.

Her problems are my problems. | We're so upset! | Great clothes, great music. | She's awful. | Tell us what's true! | Really good-looking boys

1. I think 'Really good-looking boys' is the title for Kelly's text.
2. *Go on, please.*

5 Speaking: Do you know …?

Work with a partner. Ask questions.

A: Do you know a British band that is very popular in Germany?
B: Yes, I do. I think … are popular now. Do you know a German singer that …?
A: Yes, I do. *Go on, please.*

a British band/is popular in Germany?
a German singer/is very popular?
the song/is number 1 this week?
a group/split this year?
the names of the boys/sing in …?
a DJ/plays good music?
…/…

6 Listening with DJ Dan: Young people and music

Dan is talking to some young people about music.
Listen and take notes.
What problems have Mark, Lisa and Scott got?

name	problem
Mark	…
Lisa	…
…	…

7 Writing: A letter to a magazine

Write to a magazine.
You can write …

… a fan letter about a band or a singer. Why are they so great?

or you can write …

… a letter that says why you don't like a group or a singer. Why are they so awful?

8 A song: She left me

Fletcher, Thomas Michael/Bourne, James Elliot

Listen to this song. It's by McFly.

She walked in and said
She didn't wanna know anymore.
Before I could ask why
She was gone out the door.
I didn't know, what I did wrong,
But now I just can't move on.

Since she left me,
She told me
Don't worry,
You'll be OK, you don't need me.
Believe me you'll be fine!
Then I knew what she meant,
And it's not what she said,
Now I can't believe that she's gone.

she didn't wanna know anymore – *sie wollte nichts mehr hören;* just – *einfach;* move on – *weitermachen;* since – *seit;* Don't worry – *Mach' dir keine Sorgen;* what she meant – *was sie meinte*

Project: Profile of a band

Make a profile of a band. You can work alone or in small groups.

The band can be:

a famous one like the Beatles
your favourite band
a band in your town
an orchestra
...

Your profile can look like this:

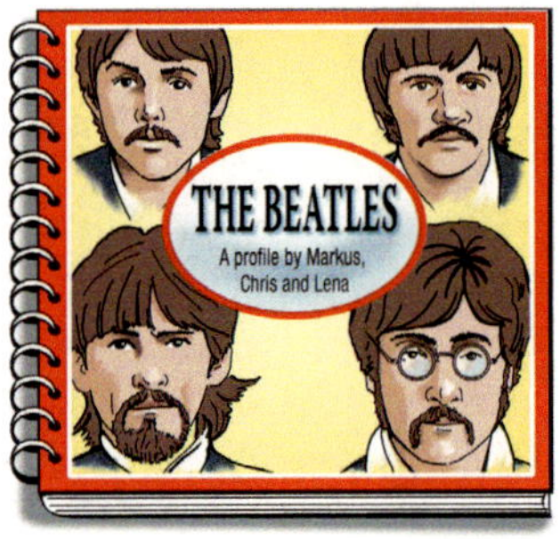

1. *Decide which band you would like to write about. Find information about the band and pictures.*

2. *Here are some ideas for the pages of your profile. Use the information and the pictures that you found. The profile should also have a cover.*

Style of music and songs
What is the band's style of music? What are the band's best or most famous songs?

People in the band
Who plays which instrument? Who is / are the singer(s)? Find information about the people in the band and pictures of them.

History of the band
When did the band start? Did the band have a different name? Has anybody left the band? Can you find older pictures of the band?

CDs
What are the titles of the band's CDs? When did they make the CDs? (You can also give the CDs grades, 'A' for very good and 'E' for awful.)

Websites
Make a list of some of the websites about the band. Write a short text about the best or worst websites. Have they got interesting information? Do the links work?

3. *When you have all finished your profiles you can have a book party in the classroom. (Maybe you can send an invitation to your Music teacher!) Tell the other groups what you think is good/not so good about their profiles.*

Checklist

Ich kann	
… sagen, dass ich selbst Musik mache.	I play an instrument.
… sagen, wie oft ich übe.	I practise every week.
… sagen, welche Musik ich gut finde.	I totally love Javine. She's my favourite singer.
… sagen, wie ich Musik höre.	I've got an MP3 player that can play 20,000 songs.
… jemanden nach seinen musikalischen Interessen fragen.	Who's your favourite singer?
… sagen, warum ich eine Band gut finde.	I really like their lyrics. They understand my problems.
… fragen, ob eine Band bekannt ist.	Are they popular?

Strategy: Speaking

Freies Sprechen in einer Fremdsprache ist oft schwieriger als Lesen und Schreiben. Hier gibt es ein paar Tipps und Tricks, die dir dabei helfen können:

Wenn du vor der Klasse sprichst:

- *Benutze kurze, einfache Sätze. Packe nicht zu viel in jeden Satz hinein. Drei kurze Sätze sind besser als ein langer Satz.*

- *Während der Vorbereitung musst du deinen Text so oft wie möglich laut üben. Am besten übst du vor dem Spiegel.*

Wenn du mit anderen sprichst:

- *Wenn du jemanden nicht verstanden hast, kannst du um Hilfe oder Wiederholung bitten.*

What does this word mean?

Can you say that again, please?

Can you speak more slowly?

- *Überlege, bevor du sprichst. Wenn du mehr Zeit brauchst, kannst du die folgenden Lückenfüller verwenden.*

That's a very good question.

Just a minute, please.

Hm ….

Let me think for a minute.

Crazy weather

a

January

Yesterday the temperature in Scotland was 16 degrees. It was the warmest day in January that people can remember.

March

After a very warm winter, snow fell in many parts of the UK yesterday. Thousands of drivers had to sleep in their cars. There will be more bad weather until next week.

Will this be our hottest summer? The temperature at London Airport is almost 38 degrees today. This is great for tourists. But it must rain soon, or many towns and villages will have no water.

July

1 Headlines!

Match the headlines with the stories.

A summer like no other
Thousands of drivers can't leave their cars
A tornado comes to the south coast
Floods in many parts of the country
Warmest day in winter

1. The first headline goes with July.
2. The second headline … .
   Go on, please.

2 Through the year

Make sentences.

1. Jan./temperature/Scotland/16 degrees
   In January the temperature in Scotland was 16 degrees.
2. Mar./snow/many parts/UK
   Go on, please.
3. Jul./temperature/London Airport/almost 38 degrees
4. Oct./shops and houses/under water
5. Nov./tornado/south coast/England

I've never seen so much rain. The town centre is under water. Houses are under water. Shops are under water. The river is now five metres higher than it should be. And there will be more rain and floods tomorrow.

October

November

NEWS

Weather

Last night a tornado came to the south coast of England. The wind destroyed houses, trees and a campsite. There has never been a storm like this in the UK.
Click here for more stories.

Internet

Say it!

There **will be** more bad weather until next week.	*Das Wetter **bleibt** bis nächste Woche schlecht.*
The temperature **is** 38 degrees today.	*Heute **haben wir** 38 Grad.*

3 Listening: The weather report

What will the weather be like in England, in Scotland and in Wales?
Listen and take notes.

England	Scotland	Wales
…	…	…

4 Speaking: Crazy weather?

What crazy weather can you remember?
Make notes. Then tell the class about your crazy weather.

the warmest/coldest/… that I can …
the temperature was …
never seen so much …
… was under water
… had to …
…

b Boscastle is a small village in Cornwall. On Monday, 16th August 2004 it suddenly started to rain in Boscastle.

Boscastle is in a valley near the sea. Many tourists visit the popular Museum of Witchcraft in the village.

Say it!

If it **rains**, we'**ll need** our anoraks.	*Wenn es **regnet**, **brauchen** wir unsere Anoraks.*
If it **rains** tomorrow, we **won't stay** here.	*Wenn es morgen **regnet**, **bleiben** wir **nicht** hier.*

5 That's wrong!

1. Boscastle is in a valley near a lake.
   That's wrong! It's in a valley near the sea.
2. It hasn't got a museum.
   Go on, please.
3. If it's sunny, the tourists will need their anoraks.
4. The anoraks are at the beach.
5. If the weather is better tomorrow, they'll go to a café.
6. If it rains again, they'll go to the Museum of Witchcraft.
7. If they go to the café, they can find out about witchcraft.

6 Speaking: Weekend plans

a) What will you do at the weekend? *Make two lists.*

go on a camping trip
play football
...

stay at home
go to the leisure centre
...

b) *Make dialogues with a partner.*

A: What will you do at the weekend?
B: If the weather is nice, I'll go on a camping trip.
A: And if it rains?
B: If it rains, I won't go on a camping trip. I'll ... then.

c Andrew Williams is a pilot. On 16th August his helicopter flew to Boscastle.

"We left at four o'clock. I flew the helicopter myself. The storm was very bad. We saw that the village was under water. People were on their houses and in trees. Some stood on cars, but the water carried the cars into the sea. It was a disaster."

The pilots saved about 60 people. They pulled people out of houses and out of trees. Many people tried to save themselves. One girl pulled herself from the river.

Kate:

I was in Boscastle with my parents. I saw the disaster myself. The water destroyed cars, houses, shops. There were pets in some of the cars. It's a pity that we couldn't save them. You feel angry with yourself because you can't help them.

Say it!

Many people tried to save **themselves**.
*Viele Menschen versuchten, **sich** zu retten.*

I saw the disaster **myself**.
*Ich habe die Katastrophe **selbst** gesehen.*

7 A disaster

A reporter has made some notes about the disaster.
Write what happened.

On August 16th there was a very bad storm in … . *Go on, please.*

August 16th – a very bad storm
so much rain – village under water
people on houses / in trees / on cars –
4 o'clock – helicopters – flew to village –
pulled people from trees – couldn't save pets – …

8 Speaking: Do you do it yourself?

a) *Make two lists.*

do it myself	don't do it myself
…	…

do my homework   make my bed
tidy up …   repair …
buy …   cook …
…

b) *Talk about your lists with a partner.*

A: I always do my homework myself. And you?
B: I usually do it myself. But my brother sometimes helps me with Maths.
I always make my bed myself.
Do you do that yourself, too?
A: Go on, please.

Before you read:
Look at page 67 again. Who is Kate Benson and why was she in Boscastle?
Then look at the pictures here. What did Kate do when the water came?

The storm

Kate Benson, her older sister Susie and their parents were in Boscastle. It was August, and it was a rainy afternoon. They left their car in the car park and walked into the village. All the tourists wore anoraks as they walked in and out of the shops and cafés. Some went down the road to the sea. Others came slowly back.

"What would you like to do?" asked Kate's mother.
"It's so boring," said Susie.
"It's still raining," said Kate's father. "Should we drive back to the cottage?"
"We can wait here until it stops," said Kate's mother.
Suddenly Susie said, "Let's go to the Museum of Witchcraft. That'll be cool."
"OK," said Kate's mother. "You two can go in there and we'll look at the shops."

Kate and Susie went into the museum. They looked at the exhibition. The museum was dark. Outside they could hear the storm and the rain.
"Listen to the storm," said Susie. "The witches are coming. Look."
Kate saw a model of a witch in black clothes and with a black hat.
"She'll come through your bedroom window in the night," said Susie.
"Stop it," said Kate.
Suddenly, a window broke.
Kate was so scared, she screamed.
Then a door broke. People started to shout and scream as water came into the museum. It came through the door and windows.
"What's happening?" screamed Kate.
"I don't know," said Susie.

There was lots of water in the museum now. Parts of the exhibition fell into the water. Outside there was a large river between the houses and shops. It carried cars, trees, tables, boxes through the village to the sea. People tried to climb away from the water.
Kate suddenly screamed. A dead woman was in the water. Kate saw her black hair and the black clothes.
"It isn't a woman," shouted Susie. "It's the model of the witch from the museum."

The water in the museum was now very high. Kate and Susie climbed the stairs. As they climbed, the water followed them. Suddenly they heard a loud noise outside. They ran into a room and opened a window. They saw helicopters over the village. A helicopter flew over the museum where Kate and Susie were. A line came down from the helicopter. A man in a uniform came down with the line.

"Come quickly," said the man.

The man took Kate and the pilot pulled her up to the helicopter.

In the helicopter she saw her parents. They were cold and wet.

Then the man went down again and saved her sister.

"You were very lucky," said the man in the uniform. "Your parents saw you."

As they all looked out of the helicopter, a shop near the museum fell into the water.

Later in the evening Kate and Susie were with their parents in their holiday cottage and saw pictures of Boscastle on TV.

"This is just like a disaster film," said Kate's father. "But it happened and we were all in it."

1 Titles

Match a title with a part of the story.

I think 'A rainy afternoon' is a good title for the … part of the story.

- Just like a film
- So boring!
- A dead woman?
- Water came through the windows and doors
- Helicopters arrived
- A rainy afternoon

2 An interview

After the disaster lots of reporters came to Boscastle. One reporter spoke to Kate.

a) *Act dialogues with a partner. One of you is the reporter. The other is Kate.*

A: Can I ask you some questions about the disaster in Boscastle?
B: Yes, of course.
A: Where were you …?
B: I can remember that quite well. I was … .

- Where were you when the disaster started?
- What happened?
- How did you feel when the water …?
- What was the worst …?
- Were you scared when …?
- How … your parents?

b) *Now write the interview.*

1 Parents and children

Children often have to help their parents. *Make sentences.*

1. you – help in the kitchen / I – cook your favourite meal
   If you help in the kitchen, I'll cook your favourite meal.
2. you – want a sandwich / I – make one for you
3. you – tidy up your room / we – watch a DVD together tonight
4. you – don't tidy up your room / we – watch it without you
5. you – don't do that Maths homework / your teacher – be angry
6. you – work hard for your Geography test / you – get a better grade
7. you … / I …

2 Speaking: No, thank you!

Kate and Susie/cook a curry

Simon/make a cake for a party

Lisa and Tom/repair Tom's bike

Ben/write his History project

Helen/book a flight

I	myself
you	yourself
he	himself
she	herself
we	ourself
they	themselves

Make different dialogues.
You can act a dialogue like this:

A: What are Kate and Susie doing?
B: They're cooking an Indian curry.
A: Should we help them?
B: No. They can cook it themselves.

or like this:

A: Hi, Kate. What are you doing?
B: Hi. We're cooking a curry.
A: Can I help you?
B: No, thank you. We can cook it ourselves.

3 Listening: Different people

Four different people are talking about the Boscastle disaster.
Who are the speakers? Which words tell you? Take notes.

1. First speaker: … . Words: …
2. *Go on, please.*

a teacher
somebody that has got a shop
a reporter
a taxi driver
somebody that lives in the village
a tourist

4 A picture story

Look at the pictures. Tell the story. Find your own ending.

One day in August, Sue Brown and her parents visited Boscastle.
They parked their car … . *Go on, please.*

5 The 'If …' game

a) *Work in a group. Everybody writes the first part of a sentence with 'If …'.*
Give it to the next player, but he/she mustn't see the sentence.
This player finishes the sentence.

b) *Now read your sentences to the group.*

If you give me 10 euros,

I'll push you into the river.

If you give me your phone,

I'll cook it for lunch.

6 Mediation: Fire

You're in a hotel with a group of German tourists. One of the tourists can't speak English and asks what this sign says.
Tell the tourist about the sign in German.

- Was sollte man zuerst tun, wenn es brennt?
- Sollte man zuerst seine Wertsachen holen?
- Wo sollte man hingehen?
- Sollte man zurückgehen?
- Was soll man dabei einschlagen?

TIPP

Arbeiten mit dem Wörterbuch IV

Ein Wörterbuch kann sehr hilfreich sein. Aber Vorsicht! Nicht immer ist die erste englische Bedeutung die richtige! Schaue dir immer alle Bedeutungen an, bevor du dich für eine entscheidest.

Ein Beispiel: Du willst sagen, dass du vergessen hast, deinen Wecker zu stellen. Du wirst merken, dass „stellen" in deinem Wörterbuch ganz unterschiedliche Bedeutungen hat. Welche ist die richtige? Lies weiter und du findest in den meisten Wörterbüchern einen speziellen Eintrag zu deiner Frage, z. B. „den Wecker ~ set the alarm". Dein Satz heißt demnach „I forgot to set the alarm." Probier dasselbe einmal mit den markierten Wörtern aus. Welches ist die richtige Bedeutung?

1. Ich schlage ihn im Tennis immer. (schlagen)
2. Er hat den Ball nicht getroffen. (treffen)
3. Deine Hose sitzt gut. (sitzen)

7 Word web: Weather

Make a word web for 'weather' in your exercise book.

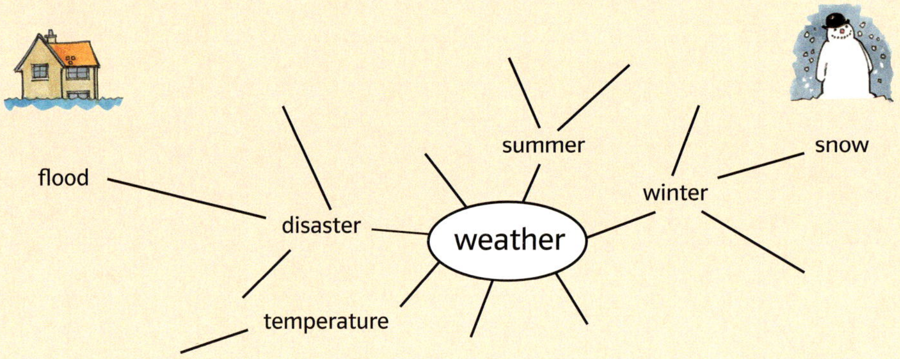

8 Weather friends

Find pairs.
1. rain – anoraks
2. *Go on, please.*

anoraks • rain • tornado • degrees
flood • summer • snow • too much water
winter • temperature • warm • destroy

9 Listen and speak

Read these sentences. Put the words with 'th' in two groups.

1. Does **the** hot wea**th**er make you **th**irsty?
2. **Th**ink of **th**ree **th**ings **th**at start with 'th'.
3. **Th**row **th**ese Ma**th**s books into the box. **Th**ank you.
4. On **th**e **th**ird **Th**ursday of **th**is mon**th**, fa**th**ers and mo**th**ers can see ano**th**er school play.

[ð]	[θ]
the	thirsty
weather	…
…	

10 What's the weather like?

Talk about the weather.

1. The weather in London is sunny. The temperature is 24 degrees. That's warm!
2. The weather in Edinburgh is … .
   Go on, please.

London	Edinburgh	Cardiff	Berlin	New York	Your town
24°	17°	20°	18°	32°	?°

11 The wrong word

What's the wrong word?

1. hot, busy, warm, cold
   The wrong word is 'busy'.
2. pilot, witch, teacher, caretaker
   Go on, please.
3. valley, mountain, coast, headline
4. fire, wind, rain, snow
5. car, helicopter, bus, van
6. storm, tornado, flood, cloudy
7. river, field, lake, sea
8. bad, high, wide, long

12 Let's go to Cornwall!

Some words are wrong here. What's right?

1. Let's go to Cornwall next **winter**.
   Let's go to Cornwall next summer.
2. The weather will be **cold** there.
   Go on, please.
3. We can stay at the **old** campsite.
4. The campsite is **more expensive** than a hotel.
5. It's got a **big** swimming pool.
6. We mustn't **remember** our tent!
7. We'll have a **bad** holiday.

13 A cartoon

It must be summer, the rain's warmer.

14 A poem: Bad weather

a) *What's missing?*

I'm always upset
When it's cold and … .

It isn't funny
When it's too hot and … .

When there's snow
I think 'Oh, …!'

And when there's ice
It isn't … .

I almost never
Like the …!

b) *Listen and check your answers.*

poem – *Gedicht*; ice – *Eis*

If-clauses *(Bedingungssätze)*

Verwendung:
Du verwendest if-Sätze, um zu sagen, unter welcher Bedingung etwas geschehen wird.

If it rains, we'**ll need** our anoraks.
If it's sunny, we'**ll leave** them here.

Bildung:
Im Bedingungssatz mit if *steht das* present simple, *im Hauptsatz das* will-future.

If somebody **comes** with me, **I'll go** to the cinema tonight.
If we **don't go** now, we **won't be** there on time.

Achtung!
Im Deutschen wird in Bedingungssätzen nur die Gegenwart verwendet.

If they **stay** another week, I'**ll leave**!

Welcher Beispielsatz passt zu Cartoon A? Warum?

Reflexive pronouns *(Reflexivpronomen)*

Verwendung:
Du verwendest die Reflexivpronomen
- *um zu sagen, dass jemand etwas selbst gemacht hat.*
- *wie das deutsche Wort ‚sich'.*

I did it **myself**.

They tried to save **themselves**.

Bildung:
Singular: -self
Plural: -selves

I →	my**self**	we →	our**selves**
you →	your**self**	you →	your**selves**
he →	him**self**	they →	them**selves**
she →	her**self**		

Welcher Beispielsatz passt zu Cartoon B? Warum?

Checklist

Ich kann	
… über das Wetter sprechen.	The temperature is 38 degrees today!
… sagen, wie das Wetter werden wird.	There will be more rain next week.
… sagen, was ich mache, falls das Wetter schlecht wird.	If it rains again tomorrow, we won't stay here.
… sagen, was ich mache, falls das Wetter gut wird.	If the weather is better tomorrow, we'll go to the beach.
… sagen, was ich immer selbst mache.	I always do my homework myself.
… sagen, was jemand für/mit sich selbst getan hat.	They tried to save themselves.
… von einem Ereignis berichten.	On August 16th there was a very bad storm in Boscastle.

Checkout: Help us to help the environment!

THE GREEN VILLAGE HOTEL

Dear guest,
Many tons of detergents and water are wasted every day to wash towels that have only been used for a short period of time. We would be grateful if you could help us to do something against this! Please help us to protect our environment by using your towels twice. Thank your very much for your help!
Have a pleasant stay!

The Green Village Hotel Management

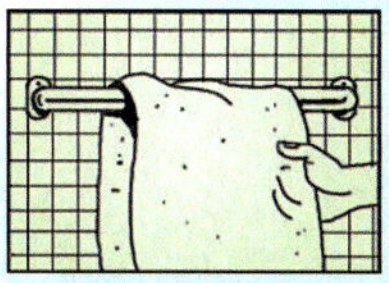

If you want to use your towels again, just leave them on the towel rack.

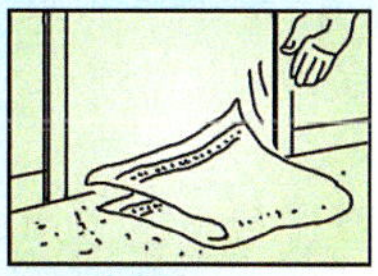

If you want new towels, just put them on the floor in front of your door.

Was würdest du mit deinen Handtüchern machen? Hier gibt es wie immer einige Wörter und Wendungen, die du nicht kennst. Du kannst sie aus dem Zusammenhang erschließen oder in der alphabetischen Wortliste ab S. 107 nachschlagen.

TIPP

Tipps: Help us to help the environment!

1. are wasted: *Dies ist eine Verbform im Passiv. Das heißt, es wird etwas mit einer Sache gemacht.*
2. by using: *Hier wird konkret vorgeschlagen, wie man helfen kann.*
3. towel, towel rack: *Versuche diese Wörter aus dem Zusammenhang zu erschließen. Du siehst sie auch auf den Bildern.*

Top sports

a We asked some young people about their favourite sports and activities. Here are their answers.

Say it!

It's exciting, but it's also dangerous.	*Es ist aufregend, aber auch gefährlich.*
I prefer to be active.	*Ich bin lieber aktiv.*

1 Sports and activities

a) *Think of sports and activities. Put them in these groups. Some sports and activities can go into more than one group.*

b) *Can you think of other groups for sports and activities?*

spectator sports	**leisure activities**
Formula One	darts
…	…

extreme sports	**team sports**
bungee jumping	football
…	…

karate

Helen, Abergavenny

Formula One

ice skating

2 Speaking: Your sports

Ask a partner.

A: What's your favourite spectator sport?
B: I like … because … .
A: Do you like extreme sports?
B: Yes, I do. I like … because … . /
No, I don't. I hate them because … .

spectator sports   leisure activities
extreme sports   team sports

3 Speaking: Sports results

Look at the sports page of a newspaper. What sports results can you find from the UK? Tell the class.

There was a … game / race / competition in … yesterday.
… won. …

b Are you an active type or are you a couch potato? Do you jump on a skateboard or do you sit in front of the TV in your free time? This quiz will show you how active you are.

A quiz

Which type are you?

1. You've got some free time. What do you do?
a) Listen to music and dance
b) Watch TV or play computer games
c) Do sports or go to training

2. How often do you do sports?
a) More than once a week
b) Once a week
c) Only at school

3. You're with a friend. What do you prefer to do?
a) Go where you can dance / talk
b) Go to the cinema
c) Go swimming

4. It's the weekend. Do you sleep until …
a) 8 o'clock?
b) 9 o'clock?
c) 1 o'clock?

5. Which of these clubs would you like to join?
a) A club like the film club
b) A sports club where you're always active
c) A music club or an art club

6. Which of these questions can you always answer?
a) Did you / your team win the last game?
b) How did that detective story finish?
c) Who won the football game on TV?

7. You've got some money for your birthday. What would you like to buy?
a) New trainers
b) A new DVD, CD or computer game
c) A football, a basketball or a skateboard

8. Which of these holidays do you prefer?
a) A beach holiday where you can swim
b) An activity holiday with lots of sport
c) A holiday where you can be very lazy

4 Active type or couch potato?

Check your partner's answers. Tell him / her about the results.

How many points?			You can say:
1. a) 5	b) 0	c) 10	55–80 points: Congratulations!
2. a) 10	b) 5	c) 0	You're very active. You enjoy sports.
3. a) 5	b) 0	c) 10	
4. a) 10	b) 5	c) 0	30–50 points: You're quite active.
5. a) 0	b) 10	c) 5	But you could do more sports.
6. a) 10	b) 0	c) 5	
7. a) 5	b) 0	c) 10	5–25 points: You really should be more active.
8. a) 5	b) 10	c) 0	
			0 points: That's a pity!
			You really are a couch potato!

5 Popular sports

a) Here are the results of a survey about sports that people do in the UK.
What's missing?

1. … is the most popular sport.
2. … go swimming.
3. … do yoga and … .
4. … isn't very popular. Only … do that.

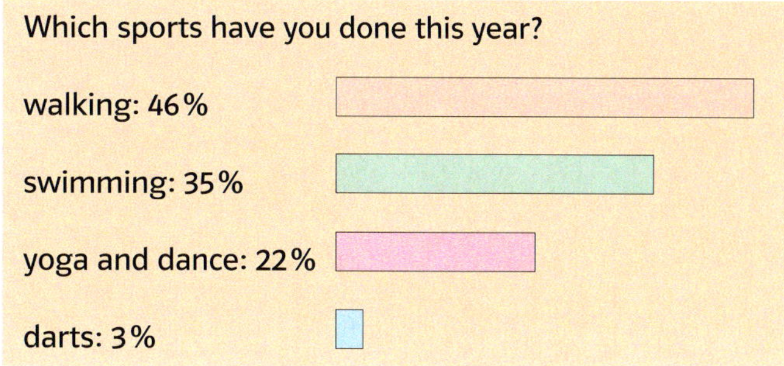

b) *Find a survey like this for Germany. Are different sports popular?*

6 Listening with DJ Dan: Which sports?

Dan and his callers are talking about sports.
What do Gemma, Ben, Nicky and Scott do? Take notes.

	Gemma	Ben	…
sport?	tennis	…	
when?	every Tuesday	…	
where?	…		
how good?			

7 Writing: Your favourite activity

Write about your favourite sport or leisure activity. First make notes.

- What's your favourite sport or activity?
- How often do you do it?
- Do you go to a club?
- Are you in a team?
- Do you go to training? If you go to training, when?
- Have you ever won anything?

8 A song: We are the champions

Mercury, Freddy

I've paid my dues, time after time.
I've done my sentence,
But committed no crime.
And bad mistakes,
I've made a few,
I've had my share of sand
Kicked in my face,
But I've come through.

We are the champions, my friends,
And we'll keep on fighting till the end.
We are the champions,
We are the champions,
No time for losers,
'Cause we are the champions
Of the world.

dues – *Lehrgeld;* time after time – *immer wieder;* do my sentence – *meine Strafe absitzen;* commit – *begehen;* crime – *Verbrechen;* mistake – *Fehler;* a few – *ein paar;* share – *Anteil;* sand – *Sand;* I've come through – *ich habe es geschafft;* we'll keep on fighting – *wir werden weiterkämpfen;* till – *bis;* loser – *Verliererin, Verlierer;* 'cause – *weil;* world – *Welt*

Project: Sports clubs

Work in groups. Write a profile of a sports club you know and present it to the class. You can make a poster or a presentation. Here are some ideas for your work:

- What do you know about the history of the club? How old is it?
- What's the sport like? Is it dangerous, extreme, popular, boring? Can you show the sport to the class?
- Is it difficult to join the club? How many people are in the club? How much does it cost?
- Has the club got any famous players? Which competitions has the club won?
- Do you like the club and the sport? Why or why not?

As always, organize your work in four steps:

1. *Plan the work! (Which club? Who does what?)*
2. *Do the work! (Find information and pictures, write texts and make a poster.)*
3. *Present the work! (Show your poster to the class or give your presentation.)*
4. *Talk about the project! (What was good? What can you do better next time?)*

Checklist

Ich kann	
… sagen, dass etwas aufregend, aber gefährlich ist.	It's exciting, but dangerous.
… sagen, dass ich eine bestimmte Sportart immer schaue.	I always watch Formula One on TV.
… sagen, was mir lieber ist.	I prefer to be active.
… jemandem gratulieren.	Congratulations!
… jemanden fragen, ob er Sport treibt.	Do you do sports?
… jemandem nach seinem Lieblingssport fragen.	What's your favourite sport?
… jemanden fragen, wie oft er einen Sport betreibt.	How often do you go swimming?

Strategy: Listening

Das Hören von englischen Texten kann man üben. Die folgenden Tipps können dir dabei helfen. Probiere sie mit dem Text ‚Gemma and Helen on the phone' aus, den du auf der CD im Workbook findest.

A Vor dem Hören

- *Mache dir klar, um was für eine Art von Text es sich handelt (ist es z. B. ein Telefongespräch, ein Fernsehbericht oder eine Erzählung?).*
- *Finde heraus, wer mit wem über was spricht.*
- *Überlege, was du über das Thema bereits weißt und was du von dem Text erwartest.*

B Während des ersten Hörens

- *Mache dir keine Notizen, entspanne dich und höre einfach nur konzentriert zu!*
- *Sorge für grundsätzliche Orientierung: Was passiert wo, wann und mit welchen Personen?*

C Während des zweiten Hörens

- *Mache dir Notizen in einem Hörprotokoll:*

Wer?	Was?	Warum?	Wann?	Wo?
Gemma and Helen	…	…	…	…

D Nach dem Hören

- *Fasse den Text mündlich für eine Freundin oder einen Freund zusammen. Du kannst das auf Englisch oder Deutsch tun.*
- *Falls es Fragen zum Text gibt, kannst du diese jetzt beantworten.*

Grammar

1 Questions and answers

Match the questions with the answers.

1. When do you want to go to Scotland?	We'd like to stay in a cottage.
2. How can I get to Scotland?	I totally love DJ Dan!
3. What would you like to do there?	Well, I like darts.
4. Where would you like to stay?	We'll go there in late August.
5. Have you ever been to London?	If it's sunny, we'll go swimming.
6. Who's your favourite DJ?	You can take a flight.
7. What will you do at the weekend?	Yes, we went there last year.
8. What's your favourite sport?	We'd like to climb Ben Nevis.

2 We haven't done it yet!

Make sentences.

1. we / not / book / the hotel / yet
   We haven't booked the hotel yet.
2. Tom / not / be / to London / yet   *Go on, please.*
3. look, I / find / some money / in street
4. sorry, / I / just / break / Grandma's expensive cup
5. we / not / see / Nessie / yet
6. sorry, / I / not / do / my homework / yet

3 Myself, yourself, ...

What's missing?

myself/yourself

himself/herself

ourselves/yourselves/themselves

1. Why don't you make your bed ..., Tom?
   Why don't you make your bed yourself, Tom?
2. I can't make it ... today. I haven't got time.   *Go on, please.*
3. Sally always does her Maths homework ... . Tim never does his homework ... .
4. Andrew's parents cook all the meals at the Ness House ... .
5. Can we help you? – No, thank you, we can repair the bikes ... .
6. Why don't you tidy up your rooms ..., Cathy and Ken?

4 If ...

Make sentences.

1. If she (leave) me, I (be) sad.
   If she leaves me, I'll be sad.
2. If it (be) sunny tomorrow, we (go) swimming.   *Go on, please.*
3. But if it (rain), we (not go) to the beach.
4. If Tom (not train) more, he (lose) the next race, too.
5. If you (not visit) us this evening, I (not see) you again before the holidays.

Words

5 Peter Robbins

What's the best word?

song	loudly	voice	play	download	important	orchestra
internet	practise	nervous	meet	singer	listen to	understands

Hello, my name is Peter Robbins.
I … the trumpet in our school … . We have to … every week. At home I mustn't play too … because that makes my sister … .
My girlfriend Ashley is a … . She's got a great … . At weekends we often … . We … CDs or … music from the … . Ashley really … me.
Music is very … for us! Our favourite … is 'We are the champions'.

6 Andrew

a) *Which letters are missing? Write the sentences again.*

Andrew *lw*ys w*tch*s F*rm*l* *n* r*c*s *n TV.
Th*y *r* r**lly *xc*t*ng, b*t *ls* v*ry d*ng*r**s.

b) *Make an exercise for your partner. Write a sentence from Units 5-8 without a, e, i, o and u. Your partner must write the sentence again with the right letters.*

7 What is it?

Say what the words mean in English.

1. sight: This is a famous place.
2. download *Go on, please.*
3. couch potato
4. loch
5. bed and breakfast
6. trombone
7. snow

This is a … . This means that … .
This is somebody that … .
You can see this in … .
This is a place where … .
With a … you can … . This is the same as … .
This is another word for … .

8 A presentation

Do a short presentation on one of these topics. Make notes first.

My music	Scotland	Sports
favourite band	towns and cities	favourite sport
favourite song	famous places	sports type
favourite style of music	sights	active/couch potato
CDs	nature	clubs
posters	places to stay	training
download	weather	favourite sports star
instrument	people	favourite club

Mediation

Englisch brauchst du nicht nur, um mit Engländern, Amerikanern oder Australiern zu sprechen. Du brauchst es auch, um Leuten zu helfen, die nicht so gut Englisch können. Dann kann es sein, dass du vermitteln oder übersetzen musst. Oft kann es auch passieren, dass du englische Informationen auf Deutsch weitergeben musst. All dies kannst du in den Aufgaben auf dieser Doppelseite üben.

1 Zwei Londoner Sehenswürdigkeiten (nach Unit 1)

Du bist mit deiner Klasse auf Klassenfahrt in London. In der Touristeninformation habt ihr euch einige Faltblätter von Londoner Sehenswürdigkeiten besorgt. *Arbeite mit einem Partner zusammen. Jeder von euch liest einen der beiden Texte. Erzähle deinem Partner anschließend auf Deutsch, was deine Sehenswürdigkeit so besonders macht. Überlegt dann gemeinsam, wohin ihr gehen möchtet.*

INFORMATION

TOWER OF LONDON

Go back in time at the Tower of London! The Tower is almost 1000 years old. First it was a castle for the English king. Then a part of it was an awful prison[1] for the people the king didn't like. You can see the crown jewels[2] here and the place where King Henry VIII killed[3] his second wife[4]!

The Underground station is Tower Hill. Tickets are £11.50 (children: £7.50).

MADAME TUSSAUD'S

Would you like to meet Robbie Williams, Arnold Schwarzenegger or Boris Becker? No problem! Visit Madame Tussaud's and meet many famous people there. See your favourite sports stars or stand next to your favourite actor[5]. Don't forget your camera[6] – you can take photos! Your friends at home won't see that all the famous people are really wax figures[7]...

The Underground station is Baker Street. Tickets are £9.50 (children: £6.50).

[1] prison – *Gefängnis*; [2] crown jewels – *Kronjuwelen*; [3] kill – *ermorden, töten*; [4] wife – *Ehefrau*; [5] actor – *Schauspieler, Schauspielerin*; [6] camera – *Fotoapparat*; [7] wax figures – *Wachsfiguren*

2 Loch Ness bei Nacht (nach Unit 5)

Du bist in einem Souvenirgeschäft in Schottland. Eine deutsche Frau sucht nach einem Geschenk für ihren Sohn. Sie kann kein Englisch und weiß nicht, was sie sagen soll, als der Verkäufer sie anspricht. Kannst du ihr helfen?
Arbeite mit zwei Partnern zusammen, die den Verkäufer und die Frau spielen.

Verkäufer: Can I help you?
Frau: Wie bitte? Oh je, ich suche ein Geschenk für meinen Sohn.
Du: (zu der Frau) Kann ich Ihnen helfen? (zu dem Verkäufer)…
Verkäufer: A present for her son? Does he know about Loch Ness and Nessie?
Du: …
Frau: Ja, aber er findet Nessie langweilig. Er glaubt nicht, dass es hier ein Monster gibt.
Du: …
Verkäufer: Hm, that's funny. How old is he? Does he like T-shirts with castles on them? We've got some new ones with new designs.
Du: …
Frau: Er ist 13 und trägt nur schwarze Klamotten, weil er sie cool findet.
Du: …
Verkäufer: I've got an idea. We've got very cool black T-shirts with 'Loch Ness by night' on them. Look here.
Du: …
Frau: Das ist eine gute Idee. Wie viel kosten sie?
Du: …
Verkäufer: One T-shirt is £10, but you can get two for £15.
Du: …
Frau: Super! Dann nehme ich zwei.
Du: …

3 Im Schilderwald (nach Unit 8)

Eine Fußballmannschaft aus Italien ist zu Gast bei eurem Sportverein. Ihr könnt euch nur auf Englisch mit ihnen unterhalten. Auf Ausflügen fragen sie immer wieder nach Dingen, die sie nicht verstehen. *Erkläre ihnen diese Schilder:*

1

2

3

It means that … .
You mustn't … .
You must … .
You can only … .

4

5

6

7

8

9

10

One country – or four?

The British Isles[1]

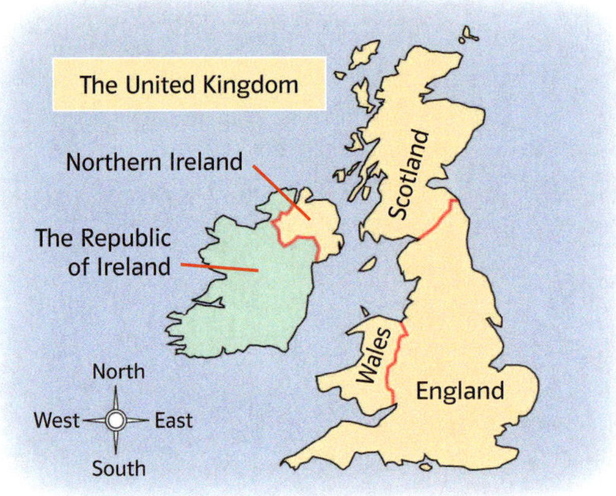

The countries of **Great Britain**[2] are England, Wales and Scotland.

The countries of **the United Kingdom** (UK) are Great Britain (England, Wales, Scotland) and Northern Ireland[3].

The countries of **the British Isles** are the UK and the Republic of Ireland[4].

 +  = the British Isles

1 How many?

1. How many countries are there in the United Kingdom? What are their names?
2. Which country is in the UK but isn't a part of Great Britain?
3. Which country is in the British Isles but isn't in the UK?
4. Which is the biggest country in the British Isles?

2 Find it!

Look at the map at the front of your book.

1. London is the capital[5] of England and the UK. Find the capitals of Wales, Scotland, Northern Ireland and the Republic of Ireland.
2. Find mountains in Scotland and Wales.
3. Find a river in the Republic of Ireland.
4. Find the part of England where there are lots of lakes.
5. Find the tunnel between the UK and France.

3 England – English

Make a list. Use your dictionary for other countries.

England Wales Russia
Italy the UK/Great Britain
Germany Ireland France
Turkey Scotland …

Irish Turkish French
Scottish Welsh English
British Russian German
Italian …

England – English
Wales – …

[1]the British Isles – *die britischen Inseln;* [2]Great Britain – *Großbritannien;* [3]Northern Ireland – *Nordirland;* [4]the Republic of Ireland – *Irland;* [5]capital – *Hauptstadt*

A dangerous place

Let's go back in time. It's the year 1600 and we're in London.

London is the biggest city in England. There are lots of people in the streets. Every day it's like a big theatre[1]: music, clowns, animals and food everywhere[2]. Men, women and children sell things in the streets. It's very loud because everybody shouts and the animals make lots of noise, too.
London is very dirty[3]. Most houses haven't got toilets or bathrooms. People throw their dirty water and rubbish[4] through their windows into the street. So if you aren't careful, something will fall on your head! People on the road to London can smell[5] the town from fifteen kilometres away. It stinks[6] awfully!
The streets are dark at night and there are many robbers[7] in London. So you should stay at home in the evening. But during the day it can also be very dangerous because there are lots of people, dogs, horses, cows and sheep on the roads. There are no police officers in London. People can run through the streets, break windows or start fires!
Almost no children go to school, so not many people can read or write. Girls can't go to school. There are some famous boys' schools in London – but they are only for boys from rich[8] families.

1 A text for the school magazine

Write a text about old London for your school magazine.

London was the biggest city in England. There were lots of people in the streets. Every day was like a big theatre: …

2 Would you like to live there?

Would you like to live in old London? *Say why or why not.*

Yes, I would because … .
No, I wouldn't because … .

no schools smelly dirty dangerous fun like a big theatre no toilets no police no cars

[1]theatre – *Theater*; [2]everywhere – *überall*; [3]dirty – *dreckig*; [4]rubbish – *Abfall*; [5]smell – *riechen*; [6]stink – *stinken*; [7]robber – *Räuber*; [8]rich– *reich*

Andrew's photos

We're picking up[1] the campervan[2] from the Bensons. My sisters aren't too happy about it, but I think it's OK.

This is my room. I always leave things until the last minute. How can I get everything into one rucksack?

We're almost ready to leave. I've just put a little surprise for my sisters in one of the beds.

Let's go! Mum is driving and Dad is reading the map. We go round and round[3] for an hour before we leave London.

We stopped here for a sandwich. A typical[4] English castle.

All the campsites are full. It's raining and raining. Our campervan hasn't got a toilet. Help!

We've decided to camp in this field. Let's hope nobody sees us. Water is coming into the campervan. Dad is trying to find the hole. Mum is shouting at him.

The next morning, Dad has repaired the hole, but we can't make tea or cook our food because there aren't any matches[5].
Dad is trying to start a fire with two sticks[6]. Mum is laughing.

We got some food in a fantastic fun park. But I'm not sure if Dad liked it. His famous last words before he got on: "Maybe I shouldn't eat a third hot dog!"

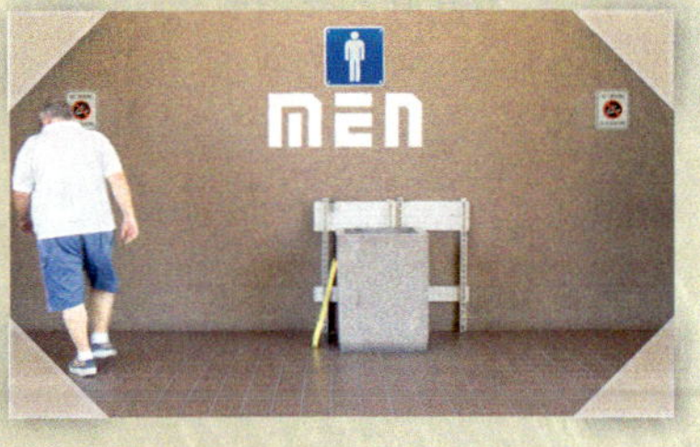

Then we didn't see him for an hour.

Cycling[7] and walking in Wales can be fun. But my bike has got a flat tyre[8] AGAIN! And all this healthy activity is too much for Mum.

"I know a faster and shorter way," Dad said on one of our walking trips. I've never seen so many sheep.

A 'traditional[9] English breakfast' — in a Welsh B&B! Fried[10] bacon[11], fried eggs, fried sausages[12], and toast. Mum calls it a 'heart attack[13] on a plate[14]'.

Three days without photos — no film in the camera!

The Jones' new house in Penryn. The campervan isn't working again, but they say that we can stay with them as long as we like!!! So Mum gets her 'hotel', Dad can relax, and the Jones have given me their tent. We go swimming and surfing every day, so it's a perfect[15] holiday!

1 How fast can you find them?

Work with a partner. Read the texts and see how fast you can find:

five animals | six things to eat | four places to sleep | four hobbies

2 Your holiday story

Write about a funny, fantastic or terrible holiday. It can be something that really happened or you can write a new story. If you want, you can also use photos.

[1]campervan – *Wohnmobil;* [2]pick up – *abholen;* [3]round and round – *im Kreis;* [4]typical – *typisch;* [5]matches – *Streichhölzer;* [6]stick – *Stock;* [7]cycling – *Fahrrad fahren;* [8]have a flat tyre – *einen Platten haben;* [9]traditional – *traditionell;* [10]fried – *gebraten;* [11]bacon – *Schinkenspeck;* [12]sausage – *Wurst, Würstchen;* [13]heart attack – *Herzinfarkt;* [14]plate – *Teller;* [15]perfect – *perfekt*

Three poems

1 Swimming ool

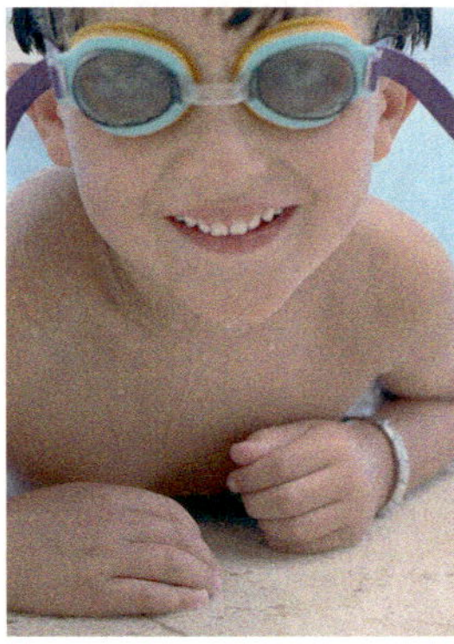

Swimming in the swimming pool
is where I like to 'B',
wearing underwater goggles[1]
so that I can 'C'.

Yesterday, before I swam,
I drank a cup of 'T'.
Now the pool's a 'swimming ool'
because I took a 'P'[2].

Kenn Nesbitt

The letters at the end of every second line are really words. Can you write the words?

Find more English words that you can write as a letter or number. Can you write a poem with them?

2 Films

Some films are sad – you watch them and cry[3].
You know that the hero[4] is going to die.
Some films have spies[5] – they fight, run and jump.
When they crash[6] their cars, there's a very big bump[7]!
Sometimes aliens[8] come down from space[9].
That often means trouble for the human race[10].
And then there are ghost films – ghosts come out at night
And give everybody an awful fright[11].
But the worst films are love films where all the stars kiss[12].
Those are the films that I want to miss!

William Sears

3 Lucky trade[13]

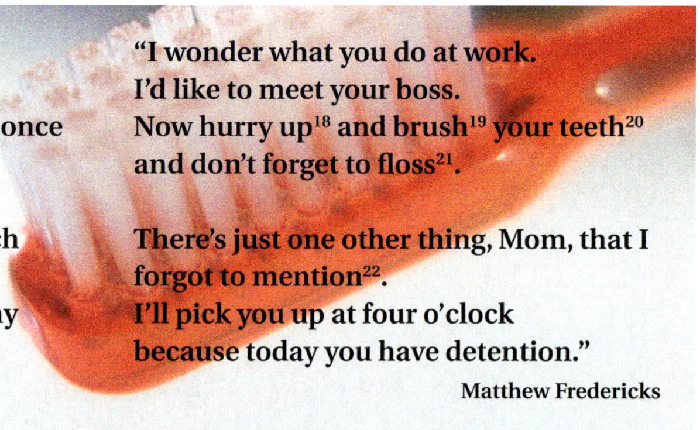

I told my mum I'd go to work
if she would go to school.
She thought that trading places[14] once
just might be kind of[15] cool.

So she agreed[16]; I packed her lunch
and made her wash her face.
Then mother said, "I wonder[17] why
you want to take my place?"

"I wonder what you do at work.
I'd like to meet your boss.
Now hurry up[18] and brush[19] your teeth[20]
and don't forget to floss[21].

There's just one other thing, Mom, that I
forgot to mention[22].
I'll pick you up at four o'clock
because today you have detention."

Matthew Fredericks

[1]goggles – *Schwimmbrille;* [2]take a pee – *pinkeln;* [3]cry – *weinen;* [4]hero – *Held/Heldin;* [5]spies – *Spione;* [6]crash – *verunglücken;* [7]bump – *Zusammenstoß;* [8]aliens – *Außerirdische;* [9]space – *das Weltall;* [10]human race – *die Menschheit;* [11]fright – *Schreck;* [12]kiss – *küssen;* [13]lucky trade – *guter Tausch;* [14]trading places – *Plätze tauschen, Rollen tauschen;* [15]kind of – *irgendwie;* [16]agree – *zustimmen;* [17]wonder – *sich wundern;* [18]hurry up – *sich beeilen;* [19]brush – *bürsten, putzen;* [20]teeth – *Zähne;* [21]floss – *Zahnseide verwenden;* [22]mention – *erwähnen*

Vocabulary

Auf den *Vocabulary*-Seiten findest du alle Wörter und Wendungen in der Reihenfolge, in der sie in *Let's go 3* vorkommen. In der linken Spalte steht das englische Wort, in der Mitte die deutsche Übersetzung und rechts ein Beispielsatz, eine Abbildung oder eine Sammelbox. Wenn du wissen willst, wie ein Wort ausgesprochen wird, schaust du in der *Alphabetical word list* ab S. 107 nach. Dort findest du alle Wörter aus *Let's go* in alphabetischer Reihenfolge und mit der Lautschrift, die dir sagt, wie die Wörter ausgesprochen werden. Hier ist eine Liste der wichtigsten Lautschriftzeichen.

Englische Laute (English sounds)

Selbstlaute (Vowels)

[ɑː]	**car**; ähnlich wie in *Bahn*
[ʌ]	**number**; ähnlich wie in *Dach*
[e]	**yes**; ähnlich wie in *nett*
[ə]	**a** pen; ähnlich wie der Endlaut in *bitte*
[ɜː]	**girl**
[æ]	**bag**
[ɪ]	**it**; ähnlich wie in *Kind*
[i]	**happy**; ähnlich wie in *Gummi*
[iː]	**see**; ähnlich wie in *tief*
[ɒ]	**on**; ähnlich wie in *Kopf*
[ɔː]	**morning**; ähnlich wie in *ohne*
[ʊ]	**put**; ähnlich wie in *Schutt*
[uː]	**you**; ähnlich wie in *du*

Doppellaute (Diphthongs)

[aɪ]	**my**; ähnlich wie in *kein*
[aʊ]	**now**; ähnlich wie in *Frau*
[eə]	**there**
[eɪ]	**say**
[ɪə]	**here**
[ɔɪ]	**boy**; ähnlich wie in *Heu*
[əʊ]	**go**
[ʊə]	**tourist**

Mitlaute (Consonants)

[j]	**yes**; wie das deutsche *j* in *ja*
[l]	**school**
[ŋ]	**song**
[r]	**ruler**
[s]	**see**; stimmloses ‚s' wie in *reißen*
[z]	**is**, stimmhaftes ‚s' wie in *brausen*
[ʒ]	**television**; wie in *Jalousie* und *Gelee*
[dʒ]	**jeans**; wie in *Dschungel*
[ʃ]	**she**; wie in *Tisch*
[tʃ]	**teacher**; wie in *deutsch*
[ð]	**this**; stimmhafter Lispellaut
[θ]	**thank** you; stimmloser Lispellaut
[v]	**video**; wie in *Wasser*
[w]	**what**

[ː]	bedeutet, dass der vorangehende Laut lang ist, z. B. you [juː]
[ˈ]	bedeutet, dass die folgende Silbe betont ist, z. B. hello [həˈləʊ]

Das englische Alphabet (The English alphabet)

a [eɪ]	**b** [biː]	**c** [siː]	**d** [diː]	**e** [iː]
f [ef]	**g** [dʒiː]	**h** [eitʃ]	**i** [aɪ]	**j** [dʒeɪ]
k [keɪ]	**l** [el]	**m** [em]	**n** [en]	**o** [əʊ]
p [piː]	**q** [kjuː]	**r** [ɑː]	**s** [es]	**t** [tiː]
u [juː]	**v** [viː]	**w** [ˈdʌbljuː]	**x** [eks]	
y [waɪ]	**z** [zed]			

Unit 1: London

8	**Notting Hill Carnival**	*(Karneval im Londoner Stadteil Notting Hill)*	
	carnival	Karneval, Volksfest	
	during	während →	We mustn't eat *during* lessons at school.
	Tower of London	*(Zitadelle in London)*	
	king	König →	
	queen	Königin →	She's the *queen* and he's the *king*.
	for . . . years	. . . Jahre lang →	We lived in London *for* 5 *years*, from 1998 to 2003.
	hundreds	hunderte, viele hundert	
	Buckingham Palace	*(Wohnsitz der britischen Königin)*	

A special family
father = **king**
mother = **queen**
daughter = **princess**
son = **prince**

	palace	Palast →	A king or queen lives in a *palace*.
	uncle	Onkel →	Your dad's brother is your *uncle*.
	sight	Sehenswürdigkeit →	A *sight* is a famous or interesting place.
	dialogue	Dialog, Gespräch	
9	**Hindu**	hinduistisch; Hindu	
	temple	Tempel →	Indian people don't usually go to a church. They go to a *temple*.

Where would you like to live?
In a house or a flat or . . .
a church,
a temple,
a palace,
a tower,
a castle?

	wedding	Hochzeit →	People marry at a *wedding*.
	excited	aufgeregt, begeistert →	I'm very *excited* because we're going to visit an exciting place.
	West End	*(Stadtteil von London)*	
	notes	Notizen →	Don't write down all the information. Just *take notes*.
	take notes	Notizen machen →	
	list	Liste →	What must we do for our project? – Let's make a *list*.
	class	Schulklasse, Klasse →	*class* = tutor group

Language

10	**London Eye**	*(das größte Riesenrad der Welt)*	
	free	kostenlos, frei →	It's *free*. Don't pay for it.
	miss	vermissen, verpassen, verfehlen	
	What's missing?	Was fehlt?	
11	**ought to**	sollte besser/sollten besser →	You *ought to* get a bigger bike.

	late	spät, zu spät →	Sorry I'm *late*.
	sentence	Satz	

Text: Let's go to the carnival!

12	**West Indian**	westindisch; Westinder/Westinderin →	The *West Indian* countries are between North and South America.

West Indian food isn't Indian food!
Es kommt nicht aus Indien, sondern von den 'West Indies'. Das sind kleine Inseln in der Karibik zwischen Nord- und Südamerika.

	change to	umsteigen nach →	Take this bus to the market, then *change to* a number 29.
	line	Linie, Zeile →	All the trains on this *line* go to Oxford Circus.
	on the train	im Zug	
	station	Haltestelle, Bahnhof →	Don't *get off* the train until it arrives at a *station*.
	phone	Telefon →	*phone* = telephone
	get off	aussteigen →	

London by Underground
Go to the **station**.
Buy a **ticket**.
Find the right **line**.
Get on the train.
Get off the train.
Change to another line.

13	**Piccadilly Circus**	*(Platz in London)*	
	demonstration	Demonstration	
	Trafalgar Square	*(Platz in London)*	
	may	dürfen, können →	*May* I open the window?
	credit	Guthaben, Kredit →	I can't phone Emily because I've got no *credit*.
	rang	klingelte/klingelten, läutete/läuteten	
	order	Reihenfolge	

Practice

14	**trip**	Fahrt, Reise	
	German	deutsch; Deutscher/Deutsche →	Kevin is *German*, and he speaks *German*. But he hasn't got a *German* name.
15	**tip**	Ratschlag, Tipp	
	match	zuordnen →	When you *match* things, you put them together.
	closed	geschlossen	
	unit	Kapitel	
	at the front	vorne	
	Big Ben	*(Glockenturm des englischen Parlamentsgebäudes)*	

Can you match the sights and the pictures?

Big Ben
Tower of London
London Eye
Piccadilly Circus
Trafalgar Square

	mediation	Sprachmittlung →	In *mediation* exercises you help somebody when they can't understand or speak English.

Words

16	**web**	Netz, Netzwerk	
	dictionary	Wörterbuch	
17	**go together**	zusammenpassen	
	magazine	Zeitschrift, Magazin →	Jack is a sports fan, so he reads sports *magazines*.
	puzzle	Rätsel	

Lerncheck Unit 1

Welche Wörter fehlen? carnival magazine sight station wedding

1. You can buy tickets for the train at the … .
2. Buckingham Palace is a famous … in London.
3. Hundreds of people go to the … and watch the processions.
4. This … has got lots of information about events in London.
5. Jenny went to her uncle's … last Saturday.

Unit 2: It's good to talk!

20	**topic**	Thema	
	Is that you?	Bist du es?	
	It's me.	Ich bin's.	
	It's Barbara.	Hier ist Barbara.	
	text	eine SMS schreiben →	Please *text* me. = Please send me a text message.
	UK (United Kingdom)	Vereinigtes Königreich	
	penny pl. **pence**	Pence *(britische Währungseinheit)* →	1p = one *penny*. 10p = 10 *pence*.
	per	pro →	
	minute	Minute →	30p *per minute* = One minute costs 30p. ⚠ 'Minute' reimt sich mit 'win it'.
	mobile	Handy →	*mobile* = mobile phone
	network	Netz, Netzwerk →	Which *network* does your mobile phone use?
	phone call	Telefongespräch, Anruf →	When you phone somebody, you make a *phone call*.
	plan	Programm	
	bill	Rechnung →	I've got a phone *bill* for £50. Can you *pay* the *bill* please, Dad?
	pay, paid, paid	zahlen, bezahlen →	

Money, money, money
This shop **sells** mobile phones.
You can **buy** mobiles here.
They **cost** a lot of money.
You must **pay** the **bill** for your phone calls.

	click	klicken	
	ring tone	Klingelton →	Do you like my new *ring tone*?

	page	Seite	
	add	addieren, hinzufügen →	When you *add* 1 and 2, you get 3.
	as	während, als →	Tara always phones her friends *as* she walks along the road. 
21	**Speak to you later.**	Bis dann. →	*Speak to you later.* = We can talk again another time.
	phone box	Telefonzelle	
22	**switch off**	ausschalten →	Remember to *switch off* the radio when you go out.
	steal, stole, stolen	stehlen	

Phones
You make a **phone call**.
You download **ring tones**.
You **switch off** your mobile in lessons.
You phone from a **phone box** when your mobile isn't working.
Short forms
phone = telephone   mobile = mobile phone

23	**be wrong**	Unrecht haben →	This is Kate's laptop. – No, you*'re wrong*. It isn't Kate's, it's Nina's.
	swim, swam, swum	schwimmen →	Mark is a good swimmer. He often *swims* for more than an hour. 
	ending	Ende, Schluss	

Project: Communication

24	**communication**	Kommunikation →	⚠ Die vorletzte Silbe wird betont.
	way	Art, Weg, Methode →	That's not the best *way* to eat an apple. 
	history	Geschichte	
	future	Zukunft →	⚠ Die erste Silbe wird betont. Sie reimt sich mit 'new'.
	presentation	Präsentation →	We've got lots of information for our *presentation* to the class.

How to say it right
Keine Angst vor der Aussprache!
Bei Wörtern, die mit '**-tion**' enden, wird die vorletzte Silbe betont:

communi**ca**tion	presen**ta**tion
infor**ma**tion	invi**ta**tion
regis**tra**tion	au**di**tion
compe**ti**tion	exhi**bi**tion

	in English	auf Englisch
25	**strategy**	Strategie, Lerntechnik

Lerncheck Unit 2

Kannst du Mini-Dialoge zusammenstellen? Ein Satz aus A passt zu einem Satz aus B.

A	B
Sorry, I must stop now.	Yes, it is. Hi, Ben.
Emma, is that you?	I haven't got any credit.
Why can't you text your mum?	I'm sorry, I'll switch it off.
How much was your last phone bill?	OK, speak to you later.
You mustn't use your mobile here.	I can't remember. My dad paid it.

Unit 3: Wales

26	**Wales**	*(Halbinsel im Westen Großbritanniens)*	
	twinned	verschwistert →	Lots of German towns are *twinned* with towns in the UK.
	Abergavenny	*(kleine Stadt in Wales)*	
	trombone	Posaune →	She's playing the *trombone*.
	welcome	willkommen	
	Welsh	walisisch; Waliser/Waliserin →	Wales is a country in the UK. People there speak the *Welsh language*.
	language	Sprache →	

Country	**Language**	Find out the names of …
Wales	Welsh/English	two **Welsh** towns.
England	English	three **English** football players.
Germany	German	four **German** castles.

27	**coal mine**	Kohlenbergwerk, Kohlengrube →	There are still some *coal mines* in Germany.
	Manchester United	*(bekannter englischer Fußballclub)*	
	against	gegen →	In this competition we must play *against* seven different teams.

Language

28	**training**	Training →	Football players have *training* every week, and the *coach* is their teacher.
	coach	Trainer →	
	concert	Konzert	

Sports and music

Simon **does sport**.	Nina **plays music**.
He **plays** football.	She **plays the** trombone.
… basketball.	… **the** drums.
… tennis.	… **the** guitar.
He **trains/has training** every day/week.	She **practises** every day/week.
His **coach** watches him.	Her **teacher** listens to her.
He plays in a **team**.	She plays in a **band/group**.
They have **games** against other teams.	They give **concerts**.

	last night	gestern Abend, gestern Nacht →	*last night* = yesterday evening
	this afternoon	heute Nachmittag →	Did you go jogging *this afternoon*? I phoned you but you weren't there.
	forget, forgot, forgotten	vergessen →	Please remember our concert next week. – OK, I won't *forget* it.
29	**Big Pit**	*(Bergbaumuseum in Wales)*	
	pit	Grube, Mine →	*Pit* is another word for 'coal mine'.
	miner	Bergarbeiter/Bergarbeiterin →	A *miner* works in a coal mine.
	grandad	Opa →	Your *grandad* is your father's or your mother's father.

	tonight	heute Abend, heute Nacht →	We're going to a concert *tonight*. It starts at eight o'clock.
	mine	Mine	

Yesterday	**today**
yesterday morning	this morning
yesterday afternoon	this afternoon
yesterday evening	this evening
aber:	
last night	**tonight**

Text: Katja and Rhodri

30	**knew**	wusste/wussten	
	Carmarthen Castle	*(Burgruine in Carmarthen)*	
	Carmarthen	*(Stadt im Südwesten von Wales)*	
	thought	dachte/dachten	
	watch	Armbanduhr →	a clock *a watch*
	before	bevor →	You should think carefully *before* you buy a pet.
	feel, felt, felt	fühlen, sich fühlen →	How do you *feel*? – I *feel* very ill.
	well	gut →	Rhodri is a good player. He plays *well*.

How you can feel

Sometimes you **feel**	well.	Sometimes you **feel**	ill.
...	great.	...	awful.
...	good.	...	bad.
...	fantastic.	...	sad.

31	**the next morning**	am nächsten Morgen →	Last Friday Tim went to a great party. But *the next morning* he felt very tired.
	greeting	Gruß	

Practice

32	**tour**	Führung, Tour →	How long is the *tour* of the castle? – It's two hours long.
33	**position**	Platz, Position →	At the end of the competition our team was in the third *position*.
	point	Punkt →	When you win a football game, you get three *points*.
	away game	Auswärtsspiel →	Oxford played against Greenwich in Oxford. For the Oxford team it was a *home game*. For Greenwich it was an *away game*.
	home game	Heimspiel →	

Lerncheck Unit 3

Welche Wörter fehlen? position well forgets grandad before

1. Luke always goes to Newtown's home games. He never ... .
2. He meets his friends ... the game starts.
3. Luke says, "Our team is in a good ... after the first five games."
4. He always sleeps ... after a good game.
5. Luke's ... played for Newtown forty years ago.

Unit 4: Is school cool?

38	**already**	schon, bereits	
39	**profile**	*(Zeugnis mit Selbstbeurteilung)* →	⚠ Das Wort *profile* reimt sich mit 'mobile'.
	be interested in	interessiert sein an, sich interessieren für →	I'*m interested in* music. = I think music is interesting.
	quite	ziemlich, ganz →	This book isn't fantastic. But it's *quite* good.
	report	Zeugnis, Bericht →	German pupils get their *reports* on the last day of the school year.
40	**detention**	Nachsitzen, Haft →	Let's go swimming after school. – I can't. I've got a *detention*.
	bully	tyrannisieren, drangsalieren →	The younger pupils are scared of Jack because he *bullies* them.
	sanction	Sanktion, Strafe	
	headteacher	Rektor/Rektorin, Schulleiter/Schulleiterin →	The *headteacher* is the most important teacher in a school.

New 'school' words
class
profile
headteacher
detention
sanction

	extra	zusätzlich; Zusatz →	Can I have *extra* chips, please?
41	**break, broke, broken**	brechen, zerbrechen →	Yesterday Ben *broke* a window. He *broke* a school rule, too!
	situation	Situation, Lage	
	wall	Wand →	Do you like the picture on my *wall*?

Project: Bullying

42	**freak**	Freak, Missgeburt →	Why are you so upset? – Somebody said to me: 'You're a *freak*.'
	get, got, got	werden →	I hope the weather will *get* better soon.

Get

You **get** lost.	You **get** a present.
… jealous.	… a prize.
… wet.	… a detention.
… upset.	

Things **get** better.
… worse.

	Childline	*(Kindernotruf in Großbritannien)*	
	organize	organisieren, koordinieren, veranstalten	
	plan	planen →	Make a plan for your project. – Yes, I must *plan* it carefully.
	present	präsentieren, vorstellen →	⚠ Die zweite Silbe wird betont (anders als bei 'a present' = Geschenk).

next time	nächstes Mal →	Oh no, we haven't got a map! – Sorry, I'll remember *next time*.

Lerncheck Unit 4

Welche Wörter fehlen? bully drink phone visit work
Benutze dasselbe Wort in beiden Sätzen.

1. I'd like a … . I always … lots of water after PE.
2. You must … harder. You can watch TV when you've finished your … .
3. A girl in our class is a … . But she doesn't … me!
4. This isn't our tutor group's first … to London. We … a museum here every year.
5. Can I use your …, please? I must … my parents now.

Unit 5: Scotland

46	**Scotland**	Schottland	
	mountain	Berg, Gebirge →	
	lake	See →	
	rain	regnen →	Was it rainy yesterday? – Yes, it *rained* all day.
	nature	Natur →	Why doesn't Matt like fields and mountains? – He isn't interested in *nature*.
	Ben Nevis	*(höchster Berg Schottlands und Großbritanniens)*	
	Nessie	*(angebliches Seeungeheuer im schottischen Loch Ness)*	
	Loch Ness	*(See in Schottland)*	
	loch	*(das schottische Wort für See)* →	This is a lake in England and a *loch* in Scotland.
	Scottish	schottisch →	Lots of people like *Scottish* music. ⚠ Das große 'S' nicht vergessen!
	ride, **rode**, **ridden**	fahren, reiten	

Where you find water

pond	
river	
lake (loch)	**der** See
sea	**die** See, das Meer

Ride – drive – go

You **ride** a bike.
… a pony.

A **driver** can **drive** a car.
… a bus.
… a taxi.

You're too young to drive.
But you can **go** by car.
Or you can go by bus or by taxi.

	route	Strecke, Route →	Let's go this way. It's the quickest *route* to the lake.
	Edinburgh	*(Großstadt in Schottland)*	
47	**person**	Person →	⚠ Die erste Silbe wird betont.
	bed and breakfast (B & B)	Zimmer mit Frühstück, Frühstückspension	
	youth hostel	Jugendherberge →	On our class trip we stayed in a *youth hostel*.
	cottage	Hütte, Häuschen, Ferienwohnung →	a *cottage* = a small house. There are lots of pretty *cottages* in the village.

Places to stay
tent
youth hostel
bed and breakfast
cottage
holiday flat
hotel

Language

48	**guest**	Gast →	How many people are staying in your hotel? – We have 38 *guests* right now.
	been	gewesen	
	come	gekommen	
	order	bestellen →	Would you like to *order* your meal now? 
	made	gemacht, getan	
	taken	gebracht, genommen	
	not yet	noch nicht →	No, I have*n't* found my earring *yet*. 
	done	getan, gemacht	
	Just a minute, please.	Einen Moment bitte.	
	Superman	Supermann	
49	**lose, lost, lost**	verlieren →	Oh no, I've *lost* my bus ticket!
	eaten	gegessen, gefressen →	Where are those hamburgers? – I've already *eaten* them.
	ever	jemals	
	Have you ever been to Germany?	Bist du schon einmal in Deutschland gewesen?	

Already – not ... yet	**Ever – never**
Have you made the dinner?	– Yes, I've **already** cooked it. No, I have**n't** done that **yet**.
Have you **ever** made curry?	– Yes, I have. No, I've **never** done that.

	found	gefunden	

Text: A photo of Nessie?

50	**breathe**	atmen →	It's OK. He's still *breathing*. 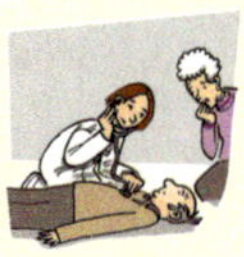
	camera	Kamera, Fotoapparat	
	could	konnte/konnten	

51	**couldn't**	konnte nicht/konnten nicht →	Why didn't you play in our team? – I *couldn't* find my trainers.
	head	Kopf	
	through	durch →	You can see *through* a window.
	model	Modell, Nachbildung →	Andy makes *models* of boats. That's his hobby.
	remote control	Fernsteuerung, Fernbedienung	

Practice

53	**bought**	gekauft	

Words

55	**sound**	Laut, Ton	
	spelling	Rechtschreibung →	The word guest is easy to say, but the *spelling* is difficult.

Lerncheck Unit 5

Welche Wörter fehlen? breathe guests mountains been cottages

1. Come to the Lake Hotel and ... in the fresh air.
2. You can climb ... or swim in the lake.
3. In Scotland tourists can stay in ... .
4. Susie hasn't ... to Edinburgh.
5. Lots of our ... come to stay here every year.

Unit 6: My music

58	**heavy metal**	Heavy Metal	
	jazz	Jazz →	In our band we don't play *jazz*.
	classical	klassisch →	DJs don't usually play *classical* music.
	that	der/die/das, dem/den *(Relativpronomen)* →	Here's the CD *that* I bought yesterday.
	totally	total, völlig →	I *totally* love 'Yellow'. = I love 'Yellow' very much. ⚠ Die erste Silbe wird betont.

Great music!
I **like** jazz.
I **enjoy** pop music.
I **totally love** rock music.
I'**m crazy about** heavy metal.

	break up	sich trennen, Schluss machen →	So Brad isn't Sue's boyfriend? – No, they've *broken up*.
59	**recorder**	Blockflöte →	Listen! My sister is playing the *recorder*.
	trumpet	Trompete	
	orchestra	Orchester	
	instrument	Instrument	

What's your favourite instrument?
drums trombone
guitar trumpet
recorder

	questionnaire	Fragebogen →	Please answer the questions on this *questionnaire*. 
	remind somebody	jemanden erinnern →	This rainy weather *reminds me* of Scotland.
	read music	Noten lesen	
60	**unhappy**	unglücklich →	happy ←→ *unhappy*
	good-looking	gut aussehend →	Is Katie pretty? – Yes, she's very *good-looking*.
	believe	glauben, denken →	⚠ Die zweite Silbe wird betont.
	split, split, split	sich trennen →	Andy and Alex don't play together now. They *split* last year.
	lyrics	Liedtext	
	shocked	schockiert, erschüttert	
	interview	Interview	
	popular	populär, beliebt	

A pop star is usually good-looking.
… popular.
… cool.
… awesome.
Fans are often unhappy when groups break up.
… shocked …
… angry …
… upset …

	title	Titel, Überschrift →	The *title* of their new song is 'Crazy girl'. ⚠ Der Anfang wird wie 'ti' in 'time' ausgesprochen.

Project: Profile of a band

62	**profile**	Porträt, Profil	
	cover	Titelseite, Einband, Hülle	

Lerncheck Unit 6

Welche Wörter fehlen? unhappy popular lyrics reminds good-looking wall

1. 'Shock' is a very … band this year.
2. The singer of the band is tall and … .
3. Lots of girls have a 'Shock' poster on their … .
4. 'Their singer, Matt, is cute,' Anna says. 'He … me of my boyfriend.'
5. But her brother Peter says, 'Their … are too difficult for me.'
6. Lisa is … because she couldn't get tickets for their concert.

Unit 7: Crazy weather

64	**temperature**	Temperatur →	⚠ Die erste Silbe wird betont. 
	degree	Grad →	
	warm	warm →	It's *warm* today. – Yes, the *temperature* is 19 *degrees*.
	snow	Schnee	
	thousands	tausende, viele tausend	
	headline	Schlagzeile →	 Read this *headline*.

65	**rain**	Regen →	The weather was very rainy. = We had lots of *rain*.
	town centre	Stadtzentrum	
	flood	Überschwemmung, Hochwasser →	There are *floods* in the street.
	tornado	Tornado →	A *tornado* is a very bad *storm*.
	coast	Küste →	There are lots of nice beaches on the *coast*.
	wind	Wind	
	destroy	zerstören →	We haven't got a car now, because the tornado *destroyed* it.
	storm	Sturm	

How was the weather?

We had snow.		It was cold.	
...	rain.	...	warm.
...	floods.	...	hot.
...	storms.	...	cloudy.
...	a tornado.	...	sunny.

Language

66	**Boscastle**	*(Dorf an der Nordwestküste Cornwalls)*	
	Cornwall	*(Halbinsel und Grafschaft an der Südwestspitze Englands)*	
	valley	Tal →	There's a *valley* between two mountains.

In the country

mountain	sea
valley	coast
river	beach
lake	

	witchcraft	Hexerei	
	if	wenn, falls; ob →	*If* there's a storm tonight, we'll stay at home.
67	**pilot**	Pilot/Pilotin	
	helicopter	Hubschrauber	
	fly, flew, flown	fliegen	
	myself	selbst, ich selbst, mich selbst →	Who made this boat? – I made it *myself*.
	disaster	Katastrophe, Unglück →	A *disaster* is a very bad accident.
	save	retten →	Help! Please *save* me!
	pull	ziehen →	*Pull!*

What can you do with a box?

pull
push
put down
carry
wear

	themselves	selbst, sie selbst, sich selbst →	Some people talk to *themselves*.
	herself	selbst, sie selbst, sich selbst	

	It's a pity.	Es ist schade./Es ist bedauerlich.	
	yourself	selbst, du selbst, dich selbst →	You shouldn't talk about *yourself* all the time.

When something bad happens to somebody, you can say:
"What's the matter?"
"What's wrong?"
"Are you OK?"
"It's a pity."

Text: The storm

68	**witch**	Hexe →	a *witch* 
	dead	tot	
69	**line**	Seil, Leine →	I hope the *line* doesn't break. 
	spoke	sprach/sprachen	

Practice

70	**himself**	selbst, er selbst, sich selbst →	Must we help Luke with his homework? – No, he can do it *himself*.
	ourselves	selbst, wir selbst, uns selbst →	We made all the food for the party *ourselves*.
	speaker	Sprecher →	A *speaker* speaks.
71	**euro**	Euro	
	sign	Schild, Zeichen	

Fire Action – Verhalten bei Feuer (page 71)

operate	betätigen
fire alarm	Feuermelder
building	Gebäude
exit	Ausgang
report to	sich melden
assembly point	Sammelplatz
collect	einsammeln
personal belongings	persönliches Eigentum
re-enter	wieder hineingehen
safe	sicher
in case of	falls
fire	Feuer

Lerncheck Unit 7

Kannst du Mini-Dialoge zusammenstellen? Ein Satz aus A passt zu einem Satz aus B.

A	**B**
What will the weather be like?	I'll stay at home and watch a disaster film.
Yesterday a tornado came to England.	Yes, the water carried it into the sea.
It's a pity about the boat.	Cold, with some rain and storms.
What will you do if it rains?	Yes, I know. Helicopters saved them.
People were on houses and in trees.	That's right. It destroyed campsites at the south coast.

Unit 8: Top sports

76	**chess**	Schach →	Do you play *chess*? – Yes, I do.
	champion	Champion, Meister/ Meisterin	
	prefer	vorziehen, bevorzugen	
	active	aktiv →	Annie does sports every day. She's very *active*.
	karate	Karate →	We do *karate* at our sports club.
	darts	Darts →	Can you play *darts*?
	spectator sport	Publikumssport →	Thousands of *spectators* watch Formula One, but they don't drive those fast cars. It's a *spectator sport*.
	spectator	Zuschauer/Zuschauerin →	
	bungee jumping	Bungeespringen →	Our PE teacher does *bungee jumping*. She goes surfing, too.
77	**extreme sports**	Extremsport →	*Extreme sports* are exciting, but they are dangerous, too.
	extreme	extrem; äußerster/ äußerste/äußerstes	

So many sports

You **do** sports.
... bungee jumping.
... karate.
... PE.

You **play** darts.
... chess.
... basketball.
... football.

You **go** ice skating.
... surfing.
... swimming.

	newspaper	Zeitung	

What can you read?

a book
a comic
a magazine
a newspaper
a report

78	**type**	Typ	
	couch potato	Fernsehglotzer/Fernsehglotzerin, Couchpotato →	Switch off that TV! You're a terrible *couch potato*.
	once	einmal; einst	
	once a week	einmal pro Woche →	They do bungee jumping *once a week*, every Saturday afternoon.

How often ...?

once a week
three times a year
five times a day

join	beitreten, sich anschließen, verbinden →	I go to the karate club every week. I *joined* it last year.
won	gewann/gewannen	

Sports: Who? Where? What?

people	**places**	**events**
spectator	changing room	competition
player	sports field	race
team	sports hall	home game
coach	swimming pool	away game
champion		training

What people do

They practise.
... train.
... join a club.
... hit a ball.
... kick ... .
... throw ... .
... run.
... jump.
... win a game.
... win a prize.

	congratulations	Glückwunsch	
79	**won**	gewonnen	

Project: Sports clubs

80	**as**	wie →	*As* always, you've finished your meal first.
	step	Schritt	

Lerncheck Unit 8

Welche Wörter fehlen? champions joined newspaper prefer spectators

1. Hundreds of ... are watching the bungee jumping.
2. A man is taking photos for a ... .
3. Caroline is new in the chess club. She ... it last week.
4. But Frank says, "I think chess is boring. I ... basketball."
5. His favourite team often wins. They are the ... .

In dieser alphabetischen Liste ist das gesamte Vokabular von *Let's go 3* enthalten. Namen werden in einer gesonderten Liste am Ende des Vokabulars aufgelistet.
Das Zeichen ⟨ ⟩ bei einer Angabe weist darauf hin, dass das Wort zum rezeptiven Wortschatz zählt.
Wendungen, die aus mehreren Wörtern bestehen, werden meist unter mehreren Stichwörten aufgeführt.
So ist z. B. *at home* unter *at* und *home* zu finden.
Die Zahlen verweisen auf das erstmalige Vorkommen der Wörter, z. B.
act I = Das Wort kam in Band I vor.
ago II = Das Wort kam in Band II vor.
already U4, 38 = Unit 4, Seite 38

A

a [ə] ein/eine **I**
⟨a bit⟩ [ə'bɪt] ein wenig **U5,** 57
a hundred [ə'hʌndrəd] hundert **II**
about [ə'baʊt] ungefähr, circa **II**
about [ə'baʊt] über **I;** wegen **II**
accident ['æksɪdnt] Unfall **II**
act [ækt] spielen *(eine Rolle)* **I**
active ['æktɪv] aktiv **U8,** 76
activity [æk'tɪvəti] Aktivität, Tätigkeit **I**
activity centre [æk'tɪvəti 'sentə] Freizeitzentrum **I**
add [æd] addieren, hinzufügen **U2,** 20
⟨addicted to⟩ [ə'dɪktɪd tʊ] süchtig nach **U2,** 25
address [ə'dres] Adresse **II**
adventure [əd'ventʃə] Abenteuer **II**
after ['ɑ:ftə] nach **I**
after that ['ɑ:ftə 'ðæt] danach **II**
... is after you [ɪz 'ɑ:ftə 'ju:] ... verfolgt dich, ... ist hinter dir her **I**
afternoon [ɑ:ftə'nu:n] Nachmittag **II**
again [ə'gen] wieder, noch einmal **I**
against [ə'genst] gegen **U3,** 27
ago [ə'gəʊ] vor **II**
air [eə] Luft **II**
airport ['eəpɔ:t] Flughafen **II**
be **alive** [bi: ə'laɪv] am Leben sein, leben **II**
all [ɔ:l] alle, alles **I**
all evening [ɔ:l 'i:vnɪŋ] den ganzen Abend lang **I**
almost ['ɔ:lməʊst] fast, beinahe **II**
alone [ə'ləʊn] alleine **I**
Leave me alone. [li:v mɪ: ə'ləʊn] Lass mich in Ruhe. **I**
along [ə'lɒŋ] entlang **I**
alphabet ['ælfəbet] Alphabet **I**
already [ɔ:l'redi] schon, bereits **U4,** 38
also ['ɔ:lsəʊ] auch **I**
always ['ɔ:lweɪz] immer **I**
an [ən] ein/eine **I**
and [ænd] und **I**
angry ['æŋgri] zornig, wütend **I**
animal ['ænɪml] Tier **I**
anorak ['ænəræk] Anorak **II**
another [ə'nʌðə] noch einer/eine/eins; ein anderer/eine andere/ein anderes **II**
answer ['ɑ:nsə] Antwort **I**
answer ['ɑ:nsə] beantworten, antworten **I**
any ['eni] irgendwelche, irgendeiner/irgendeine/irgendein **II**
not ... any ['nɒt 'eni] kein/keine **II**
anybody ['enibɒdi] irgendjemand, jeder (beliebige) **II**
anything ['eniθɪŋ] irgendetwas **II**
Anything else? [eniθɪŋ 'els] Sonst noch etwas? **I**
not ... anything ['nɒt 'eniθɪŋ] nichts **II**
apple ['æpl] Apfel **I**
April ['eɪprl] April **I**
are [ɑ:] bist **I;** sind, seid **I**
argue ['ɑ:gju:] diskutieren, streiten **I**
arrive [ə'raɪv] ankommen **II**
art [ɑ:t] Kunst **I**
as [æz] während, als **U2,** 20
as [æz] wie **U8,** 80
ask [ɑ:sk] fragen **I**
at [æt] in, auf, an, bei **I;** um **I**
at home [æt 'həʊm] zu Hause; daheim **I**
at the weekend [æt ðe wi:k'end] am Wochenende **I**
attic ['ætɪk] Dachboden, Speicher **I**
audition [ɔ:'dɪʃn] Vorsingen, Vorspielen **II**
August ['ɔ:gəst] August **I**
autumn ['ɔ:təm] Herbst **I**
away [ə'weɪ] weg **I**
away game [ə'weɪ geɪm] Auswärtsspiel **U3,** 33
awesome ['ɔ:səm] beeindruckend, super **II**
awful ['ɔ:fl] furchtbar, scheußlich **I**

B

back [bæk] zurück **I**
Text me back. [tekst mi: 'bæk] Schreib zurück (SZ). **II**
bad [bæd] schlecht, schlimm **II**
bag [bæg] Tasche **I**
ball [bɔ:l] Ball **I**
balloon [bə'lu:n] Luftballon **I**
band [bænd] Band, Gruppe **I**
bark [bɑ:k] bellen **I**
basketball ['bɑ:skɪtbɔ:l] Basketball **I**
bathroom ['bɑ:θru:m] Badezimmer **I**
be, was, been [bi:, wɒz, bi:n] sein **I**
be alive [bi: ə'laɪv] am Leben sein, leben **II**
be interested in [bɪ: 'ɪntrəstɪd ɪn] interessiert sein an, sich interessieren für **U4,** 39
be lucky [bi: 'lʌki] Glück haben **I**
Be quiet. [bi: 'kwaɪət] Sei/Seid leise. **I**
be right [bi: 'raɪt] Recht haben **II**
be scared [bi: 'skeəd] Angst haben, verängstigt sein **II**
be wrong [bi: 'rɒŋ] Unrecht haben **U2,** 23
Have you ever been to Germany? [hæv ju: evə bi:n tʊ 'dʒərməni] Bist du schon einmal in Deutschland gewesen? **U5,** 49
beach [bi:tʃ] Strand **I**
because [bɪ'kɒz] weil **I**
bed [bed] Bett **I**
bed and breakfast (B & B) [bed n 'brekfəst] Zimmer mit Frühstück, Frühstückspension **U5,** 47

go to bed [ɡəʊ tə 'bed] schlafen gehen, ins Bett gehen **I**
bedroom ['bedru:m] Schlafzimmer **I**
before [bɪ'fɔ:] bevor **U3**, 30
behind [bɪ'haɪnd] hinter **I**
believe [bɪ'li:v] glauben, denken **U6**, 60
best [best] der/die/das beste **II**
better ['betə] besser **II**
between [bɪ'twi:n] zwischen **II**
big [bɪɡ] groß **I**
bike [baɪk] Fahrrad **I**
bill [bɪl] Rechnung **U2**, 20
bird [bɜ:d] Vogel **I**
birthday ['bɜ:θdeɪ] Geburtstag **I**
Happy birthday! ['hæpi 'bɜ:θdeɪ] Herzlichen Glückwunsch zum Geburtstag! **I**
black [blæk] schwarz **II**
blonde [blɒnd] blond **II**
blue [blu:] blau **I**
board [bɔ:d] Tafel, Anschlagtafel, schwarzes Brett **I**
boat [bəʊt] Boot, Schiff **I**
book [bʊk] Buch, Heft **I**
book [bʊk] buchen **II**
boring ['bɔ:rɪŋ] langweilig **I**
⟨both⟩ [bəʊθ] beide **U3**, 37
box [bɒks] Kiste, Schachtel **I**
boy [bɔɪ] Junge **I**
boy band ['bɔɪ bænd] Boy Group **I**
boyfriend ['bɔɪfrend] Freund **I**
break [breɪk] Pause **II**
break, **broke**, **broken** [breɪk, brəʊk, 'brəʊkn] brechen, zerbrechen **U4**, 41
break up [breɪk 'ʌp] sich trennen, Schluss machen **U6**, 58
breakfast ['brekfəst] Frühstück **I**
for breakfast [fə 'brekfəst] zum Frühstück **II**
have breakfast [hæv 'brekfəst] frühstücken **I**
break-in ['breɪkɪn] Einbruch **I**
breathe [bri:ð] atmen **U5**, 50
breathe in [bri:ð 'ɪn] einatmen **II**
British ['brɪtɪʃ] britisch **II**
broken ['brəʊkn] kaputt **I**
brother ['brʌðə] Bruder **I**
brown [braʊn] braun **I**
bull [bʊl] Stier, Bulle **I**
bully ['bʊli] tyrannisieren, drangsalieren **U4**, 40
bungee jumping ['bʌndʒi dʒʌmpɪŋ] Bungeespringen **U8**, 76
bus [bʌs] Bus **I**
by (bus) [baɪ 'bʌs] mit (dem Bus) **I**
bush [bʊʃ] Busch, Gebüsch **I**
busy ['bɪzi] beschäftigt **I**
but [bʌt] aber **I**
butter ['bʌtə] Butter **I**
button ['bʌtn] Knopf, Schaltfläche **II**
buy, bought, bought [baɪ, bɔ:t, bɔ:t] kaufen **I**
by [baɪ] von **I**
⟨by using ...⟩ [baɪ 'ju:zɪŋ] indem Sie ... benutzen **U7**, 75
by (bus) [baɪ 'bʌs] mit (dem Bus) **I**

C

café ['kæfeɪ] Café **I**
cafeteria [kæfə'tɪərɪə] Cafeteria **I**
cake [keɪk] Kuchen **I**
call [kɔ:l] rufen, anrufen **I**
caller ['kɔ:lə] Anrufer/Anruferin **I**
⟨camel⟩ ['kæml] Kamel **U1**, 19
camera ['kæmrə] Kamera, Fotoapparat **U5**, 50
camping trip ['kæmpɪŋ trɪp] Campingausflug, Campingtrip **II**
campsite ['kæmpsaɪt] Campingplatz, Zeltplatz **II**
can [kæn] können **I**
can't [kɑ:nt] nicht können **I**
car [kɑ:] Auto **I**
car park ['kɑ: pɑ:k] Parkplatz **I**
card [kɑ:d] Karte **I**
card trick ['kɑ:d trɪk] Kartentrick **I**
careful ['keəfl] vorsichtig, sorgfältig **I**
caretaker ['keəteɪkə] Hausmeister/Hausmeisterin **I**
carnival ['kɑ:nɪvl] Karneval, Volksfest **U1**, 8
carrot ['kærət] Karotte **II**
carry ['kæri] tragen **I**
cartoon [kɑ:'tu:n] Cartoon, Zeichentrickfilm **I**
castle ['kɑ:sl] Schloss **II**
cat [kæt] Katze **I**
CCTV [si:si:ti:'vi:] Videoüberwachungsanlage **II**
CD [si:'di:] CD **I**
chair [tʃeə] Stuhl **I**
champion ['tʃæmpiən] Champion, Meister/Meisterin **U8**, 77
change to ['tʃeindʒ tʊ] umsteigen nach **U1**, 12
changing room ['tʃeɪndʒɪŋ ru:m] Umkleideraum **II**
chatterbox ['tʃætəbɒks] Plappermaul **I**
cheap [tʃi:p] billig **II**
check [tʃek] prüfen, kontrollieren **II**
checklist ['tʃeklɪst] Checkliste, Kontrollliste **II**
cheese [tʃi:z] Käse **I**
chess [tʃes] Schach **U8**, 76
chicken ['tʃɪkɪn] Huhn, Hähnchen **II**
children *(pl.)* ['tʃɪldrn] Kinder **I**
Chinese [tʃaɪ'ni:z] chinesisch **II**
chips [tʃɪps] Pommes frites **II**
chocolate ['tʃɒklət] Schokolade **I**
church [tʃɜ:tʃ] Kirche **I**
cinema ['sɪnəmə] Kino **I**
city ['sɪti] Stadt, Großstadt **II**
class [klɑ:s] Schulklasse, Klasse **U1**, 9
classical ['klæsikl] klassisch **U6**, 58
classroom ['klɑ:sru:m] Klassenzimmer **I**
clever ['klevə] klug **I**
click [klɪk] klicken **U2**, 20
click on [klɪk 'ɒn] anklicken **II**
climb [klaɪm] klettern **I**
clock [klɒk] Uhr **I**
... o'clock [ə'klɒk] ... Uhr **I**
close [kləʊz] schließen **I**
⟨close⟩ [kləʊs] nahe **U3**, 37
closed [kləʊzd] geschlossen **U1**, 15
clothes [kləʊðz] Kleider, Kleidung **I**
cloudy ['klaʊdi] bewölkt, wolkig **I**
clown [klaʊn] Clown **I**
club [klʌb] Club, Verein **II**
coach [kəʊtʃ] Trainer **U3**, 28
coal mine ['kəʊl maɪn] Kohlenbergwerk, Kohlengrube **U3**, 27
coast [kəʊst] Küste **U7**, 65
coffee ['kɒfi] Kaffee **I**
have a coffee [hæv ə 'kɒfi] Kaffee trinken **I**
cold [kəʊld] kalt **I**
colour ['kʌlə] Farbe **II**
What colour is ... ? [wɒt 'kʌlər ɪz] Welche Farbe hat ... ? **I**
come, came, come [kʌm, keɪm, kʌm] kommen **I**
came out: I came out [keɪm 'aʊt] ich kam heraus/ich bin herausgekommen **II**

come from ['kʌm frɒm] kommen aus **II**
Come on! [kʌm 'ɒn] Komm!/Kommt! **I**
comic ['kɒmɪk] Comicheft **I**
communication [kəmjʊ:nɪ'keɪʃn] Kommunikation **U2,** 24
competition [kɒmpə'tɪʃn] Wettbewerb, Wettkampf, Turnier **I**
computer [kəm'pju:tə] Computer **I**
concert ['kɒnsət] Konzert **U3,** 28
congratulations [kəngrætʃʊ'leɪʃnz] Glückwunsch **U8,** 78
⟨contain⟩ [kən'teɪn] enthalten **U1,** 19
cook [kʊk] kochen **II**
cool [ku:l] prima, cool **I**
cornflakes ['kɔ:nfleɪks] Cornflakes **I**
cost, cost, cost [kɒst, kɒst, kɒst] kosten **II**
cottage ['kɒtɪdʒ] Hütte, Häuschen, Ferienwohnung **U5,** 47
couch potato [kaʊtʃ pə'teɪtəʊ] Fernsehglotzer/Fernsehglotzerin, Couchpotato **U8,** 78
could [kʊd] könnte/könnten **II;** konnte/konnten **U5,** 50
couldn't ['kʊdnt] konnte nicht/konnten nicht **U5,** 51
⟨counter⟩ ['kaʊntə] Theke **U5,** 57
country ['kʌntri] Land **II**
cousin ['kʌzn] Cousin/Cousine, Vetter **I**
cover ['kʌvə] Titelseite, Einband, Hülle **U6,** 62
cow [kaʊ] Kuh **I**
crazy ['kreɪzi] verrückt **I**
credit ['kredɪt] Guthaben, Kredit **U1,** 13
cricket ['krɪkɪt] Kricket **I**
criminal ['krɪmɪnl] Verbrecher/Verbrecherin **I**
cup [kʌp] Tasse **II**
cupboard ['kʌbəd] Küchenschrank, Schrank **I**
curry ['kʌri] Curry, Currygericht **II**
⟨cut, cut, cut⟩ [kʌt, kʌt, kʌt] schneiden **U5,** 57
cute [kju:t] süß **II**

D

dad [dæd] Papa **I**
dance [dɑ:ns] tanzen **I**
dancer ['dɑ:nsə] Tänzer/Tänzerin **II**
dangerous ['deɪndʒrəs] gefährlich **I**
dark [dɑ:k] dunkel **II**
darts [dɑ:ts] Darts **U8,** 76
daughter ['dɔ:tə] Tochter **II**
day [deɪ] Tag **I**
dead [ded] tot **U7,** 68
Dear [dɪə] Lieber/Liebe/Liebes *(in Briefanrede)* **I**
December [dɪ'sembə] Dezember **I**
decide [dɪ'saɪd] entscheiden **II**
degree [dɪ'gri:] Grad **U7,** 64
demonstration [demən'streɪʃn] Demonstration **U1,** 13
departure [dɪ'pɑ:tʃə] Abflug, Abreise **II**
⟨desert⟩ ['dezət] Wüste **U1,** 19
design [dɪ'zaɪn] Muster, Entwurf **I**
destroy [dɪ'strɔɪ] zerstören **U7,** 65
detective [dɪ'tektɪv] Kriminalbeamter/Kriminalbeamtin, Detektiv/Detektivin **II**
detective story [dɪ'tektɪv 'stɔ:ri] Kriminalroman, Detektivgeschichte **II**
detention [dɪ'tentʃn] Nachsitzen, Haft **U4,** 40
⟨detergent⟩ [dɪ'tɜ:dʒnt] Waschmittel **U7,** 75
dialogue ['daɪəlɒg] Dialog, Gespräch **U1,** 8
die [daɪ] sterben **II**
dictionary ['dɪkʃnri] Wörterbuch **U1,** 16
diet ['daɪət] Diät, Nahrung **II**
different ['dɪfrnt] verschieden, anders **I**
difficult ['dɪfɪklt] schwierig **II**
dining room ['daɪnɪŋ ru:m] Esszimmer **I**
dinner ['dɪnə] Abendessen **I**
have dinner [hæv 'dɪnə] zu Abend essen **I**
disaster [dɪ'zɑ:stə] Katastrophe, Unglück **U7,** 67
disco ['dɪskəʊ] Disko **I**
discus ['dɪskəs] Diskus **I**
DJ [di: 'dʒeɪ] Diskjockey **I**
do, did, done [du:, dɪd, dʌn] tun, machen **I**
do sports [du: 'spɔ:ts] Sport(-arten) treiben **I**
dog [dɒg] Hund **I**
dog-tired [dɒg'taɪəd] hundemüde **I**
⟨dollar ($)⟩ ['dɒlə] Dollar *(amerikanische Währungseinheit)* **U2,** 25
door [dɔ:] Tür **I**
⟨doughnut⟩ ['dəʊnʌt] Donut **U5,** 57
down [daʊn] herunter, hinunter, nach unten **II**
download [daʊn'ləʊd] herunterladen **II**
draw, drew, drawn [drɔ:, dru:, drɔ:n] zeichnen **I**
dress [dres] Kleid **II**
drink [drɪŋk] Getränk **I**
drink, drank, drunk [drɪŋk, dræŋk, drʌŋk] trinken **I**
drive, drove, driven [draɪv, drəʊv, 'drɪvn] fahren **I**
driver ['draɪvə] Fahrer/Fahrerin **I**
drums [drʌmz] Schlagzeug **I**
duck [dʌk] Ente **I**
⟨dummy⟩ ['dʌmi] Dummkopf **U5,** 57
dungeon ['dʌndʒən] Verlies, Kerker **II**
during ['djʊərɪŋ] während **U1,** 8
DVD [di:vi:'di:] DVD **I**
DVD player [di:vi:'di: pleɪə] DVD-Spieler **I**

E

earring ['ɪərɪŋ] Ohrring **II**
east [i:st] Osten **I**
easy ['i:zi] einfach **I**
eat, ate, eaten [i:t, et/eɪt, 'i:tn] essen, fressen **I**
egg [eg] Ei **I**
eleven [ɪ'levn] elf **I**
Anything **else?** [eniθɪŋ 'els] Sonst noch etwas? **I**
e-mail ['i:meɪl] E-Mail **I**
embarrassing [ɪm'bærəsɪŋ] peinlich, unangenehm **II**
more embarrassing [mɔ: ɪm'bærəsɪŋ] peinlicher, unangenehmer **II**
the most embarrassing [ðə məʊst ɪm'bærəsɪŋ] der/die/das peinlichste, der/die/das unangenehmste **II**
end [end] Ende, Schluss **I**
ending ['endɪŋ] Ende, Schluss **U2,** 23
English ['ɪŋglɪʃ] Engländer/Engländerin **I;** Englisch **II**
in English [ɪn 'ɪŋglɪʃ] auf Englisch **U2,** 24
enjoy [ɪn'dʒɔɪ] mögen, genießen **II**
⟨enter⟩ ['entə] betreten **U5,** 57

⟨environment⟩ [ɪn'vaɪərnmənt] Umwelt **U7,** 75
euro ['jʊərəʊ] Euro **U7,** 71
evening ['i:vnɪŋ] Abend **I**
all evening [ɔ:l 'i:vnɪŋ] den ganzen Abend lang **I**
in the evening [ɪn ði: 'i:vnɪŋ] am Abend; abends **I**
event [ɪ'vent] Ereignis, Veranstaltung **I**
ever ['evə] jemals **U5,** 49
Have you ever been to Germany? [hæv ju: evə bi:n tʊ 'dʒərməni] Bist du schon einmal in Deutschland gewesen? **U5,** 49
every ['evri] jeder/jede/jedes **I**
everybody ['evribɒdi] jeder **I**
exchange [ɪks'tʃeɪndʒ] Austausch **I**
exchange [ɪks'tʃeɪndʒ] tauschen, wechseln **II**
excited [ɪk'saɪtɪd] aufgeregt, begeistert **U1,** 9
exciting [ɪk'saɪtɪŋ] spannend, aufregend **II**
Excuse me. [ɪk'skju:z mi] Entschuldigung. **I**
exercise ['eksəsaɪz] Übung **II**
exercise book ['eksəsaɪz bʊk] Übungsheft **I**
exhibition [eksɪ'bɪʃn] Ausstellung **II**
expensive [ɪk'spensɪv] teuer **I**
extra ['ekstrə] zusätzlich; Zusatz **U4,** 40
extreme [ɪk'stri:m] extrem; äußerster/äußerste/äußerstes **U8,** 76
extreme sports [ɪk'stri:m spɔ:ts] Extremsport **U8,** 76
eye [aɪ] Auge **II**
⟨eye level⟩ ['aɪ levl] Augenhöhe **U3,** 37
⟨eyehole⟩ ['aɪhəʊl] Augenloch **U5,** 57
⟨eyelash⟩ ['aɪlæʃ] Wimper **U1,** 19

F

face [feɪs] Gesicht **I**
face painting ['feɪs peɪntɪŋ] Kinderschminken **I**
fair [feə] Jahrmarkt, Schulfest **I**
fair [feə] fair, gerecht **II**
fall, fell, fallen [fɔ:l, fel, 'fɔ:ln] fallen **II**
family ['fæmli] Familie **I**
famous ['feɪməs] berühmt **I**
fan [fæn] Fan **I**
fancy ['fænsi] mögen **II**
fantastic [fæn'tæstik] fantastisch, toll **I**
farm [fɑ:m] Bauernhof **I**
farm machine ['fɑ:m məʃi:n] landwirtschaftliche Maschine **I**
fast [fɑ:st] schnell **II**
⟨fat⟩ [fæt] Fett **U1,** 19
father ['fɑ:ðə] Vater **I**
favourite ['feɪvrɪt] Lieblings- **I**
February ['februri] Februar **I**
feed, fed, fed [fi:d, fed, fed] füttern **I**
feel, felt, felt [fi:l, felt, felt] fühlen, sich fühlen **U3,** 30
⟨feet⟩ [fi:t] Füße **U1,** 19
felt-tip [felt'tɪp] Filzstift **I**
festival ['festɪvl] Fest **I**
fetch [fetʃ] abholen, holen **I**
field [fi:ld] Acker, Feld **I**
fight, fought, fought [faɪt, fɔ:t, fɔ:t] kämpfen, sich prügeln **I**
film [fɪlm] Film **I**
final ['faɪnl] Finale **II**
find, found, found [faɪnd, faʊnd, faʊnd] finden **I**
find out [faɪnd 'aʊt] herausfinden **I**
find out about [faɪnd 'aʊt ə'baʊt] lernen über, erfahren über **II**
fine [faɪn] in Ordnung **I**
Fine, thanks. ['faɪn θæŋks] Danke, gut. **I**
⟨finger⟩ ['fɪŋgə] Finger **U3,** 37
finish ['fɪnɪʃ] beenden **I;** enden, aufhören **II**
fire engine ['faɪə endʒɪn] Feuerwehrauto **I**
first [fɜ:st] zuerst **II**
fish pl. **fish** [fɪʃ] Fisch **I**
fit [fɪt] fit, in Form **II**
flat [flæt] Wohnung **I**
flight [flaɪt] Flug **II**
flight number [flaɪt 'nʌmbə] Flugnummer **II**
flood [flʌd] Überschwemmung, Hochwasser **U7,** 65
fly, flew, flown [flaɪ, flu: fləʊn] fliegen **U7,** 67
⟨focus⟩ ['fəʊkəs] konzentriert blicken, fokussieren **U3,** 37
follow ['fɒləʊ] folgen **I**
food [fu:d] Nahrung, Essen **I**
football ['fʊtbɔ:l] Fußball **I**
for [fɔ:] für **I**
for … years [fɔ: 'jɪəz] … Jahre lang **U1,** 8
forget, forgot, forgotten [fə'get, fə'gɒt, fə'gɒtn] vergessen **U3,** 28
fork [fɔ:k] Gabel **II**
form [fɔ:m] Vordruck **II**
freak [fri:k] Freak, Missgeburt **U4,** 42
free [fri:] kostenlos, frei **U1,** 10
fresh [freʃ] frisch **I**
Friday ['fraɪdeɪ] Freitag **I**
friend [frend] Freund/Freundin **I**
frog [frɒg] Frosch **I**
from [frɒm] aus, von **I**
from … to [frɒm tʊ] von … bis **I**
I'm from …. ['aɪm frɒm] Ich komme aus …. **I**
Where are you from? [weər ɑ: jə 'frɒm] Woher kommst du? **I**
at the **front** [æt ðə 'frɒnt] vorne **U1,** 15
fruit [fru:t] Obst, Frucht **II**
Have **fun!** [həv 'fʌn] Viel Spaß! **II**
is/are fun [fʌn] macht/machen Spaß **I**
funny ['fʌni] komisch, lustig **I**
future ['fju:tʃə] Zukunft **U2,** 24

G

galaxy ['gæləksi] Galaxie **I**
game [geɪm] Spiel **I**
garden ['gɑ:dn] Garten **I**
gate [geɪt] Tor, Flugsteig **II**
Geography [dʒi'ɒgrəfi] Erdkunde, Geografie **II**
German ['dʒɜ:mən] Deutsch **I;** deutsch; Deutscher/Deutsche **U1,** 14
get, got, got [get, gɒt, gɒt] bekommen, kriegen **I;** kaufen **II;** werden **U4,** 42
get lost [get 'lɒst] sich verlaufen **I**
get off [get 'ɒf] aussteigen **U1,** 12
get up [get 'ʌp] aufstehen **I**
ghost [gəʊst] Geist **II**
girl [gɜ:l] Mädchen **I**
girlfriend ['gɜ:lfrend] Freundin **II**
give, gave, given [gɪv, geiv, 'gɪvn] geben, schenken **I**
Just give it to me. [dʒʌzt 'gɪv ɪt tʊ mi:] Jetzt aber her damit. **II**
glass [glɑ:s] Glas **I**

glasses [ˈglɑːsɪz] Brille **I**
go, went, gone [gəʊ, went, gɒn] gehen, fahren **I**
go ice skating [gəʊ ˈaɪs skeɪtɪŋ] schlittschuhlaufen gehen **II**
go jogging [gəʊ ˈdʒɒgɪŋ] joggen gehen **I**
go on [gəʊ ˈɒn] weitermachen, weitergehen **I**
go on a trip [gəʊ ɒn ə ˈtrɪp] einen Ausflug machen, eine Reise machen **II**
go out [gəʊ ˈaʊt] ausgehen, ausfahren **I**
go rowing [gəʊ ˈrəʊɪŋ] rudern gehen **II**
go shopping [gəʊ ˈʃɒpɪŋ] einkaufen gehen **II**
go surfing [gəʊ ˈsɜːfɪŋ] surfen gehen **II**
go swimming [gəʊ ˈswɪmɪŋ] schwimmen gehen **I**
go to bed [gəʊ tə ˈbed] schlafen gehen, ins Bett gehen **I**
go together [gəʊ ˈtəgeðə] zusammenpassen **U1,** 17
go with [gəʊ ˈwɪð] zusammenpassen mit **II**
going to [ˈgəʊɪŋ tʊ] vorhaben, werden **II**
golf [gɒlf] Golf **I**
good [gʊd] gut **I**
good-looking [gʊd ˈlʊkɪŋ] gut aussehend **U6,** 60
good at [ˈgʊd æt] gut in **I**
Good morning. [gʊd ˈmɔːnɪŋ] Guten Morgen. **I**
Goodbye. [gʊdˈbaɪ] Auf Wiedersehen. **I**
grade [greɪd] Note **II**
grandad [ˈgrændæd] Opa **U3,** 29
grandma [ˈgrænmɑː] Oma **I**
⟨grateful⟩ [ˈgreɪtfl] dankbar **U7,** 75
great [greɪt] großartig **I**
green [griːn] grün **I**
greeting [ˈgriːtɪŋ] Gruß **U3,** 31
group [gruːp] Gruppe **I**
guest [gest] Gast **U5,** 48
guinea pig [ˈgɪni pɪg] Meerschweinchen **I**
guitar [gɪˈtɑː] Gitarre **I**

H

hair [heə] Haar, Haare **II**
half past [hɑːfˈpɑːst] halb **I**
⟨half⟩ [hɑːf] Hälfte; halbe, halber, halbes **U2,** 25
hamburger [ˈhæmbɜːgə] Hamburger **I**
hand [hænd] Hand **II**
happen [ˈhæpn] passieren, geschehen **II**
What's happening? [wɒts ˈhæpenɪŋ] Was geht hier vor? **I**
happy [ˈhæpi] glücklich, froh **I**
Happy birthday! [ˈhæpi ˈbɜːθdeɪ] Herzlichen Glückwunsch zum Geburtstag! **I**
hard [hɑːd] schwierig, hart **I**
hat [hæt] Hut **I**
hate [heɪt] nicht mögen, hassen **I**
have, had, had [hæv, hæd, hæd] haben **II**
have a coffee [hæv ə ˈkɒfi] Kaffee trinken **I**
have breakfast [hæv ˈbrekfəst] frühstücken **I**
have dinner [hæv ˈdɪnə] zu Abend essen **I**
Have fun! [həv ˈfʌn] Viel Spaß! **II**
have got [hæv ˈgɒt] haben, besitzen **I**
have lunch [hæv ˈlʌntʃ] zu Mittag essen **I**
have to [ˈhæv tʊ] müssen **II**
Have you ever been to Germany? [hæv juː evə biːn tʊ ˈdʒərməni] Bist du schon einmal in Deutschland gewesen? **U5,** 49
he [hiː] er **I**
head [hed] Kopf **U5,** 51
headline [ˈhedlaɪn] Schlagzeile **U7,** 64
headteacher [hedˈtiːtʃə] Rektor/Rektorin, Schulleiter/Schulleiterin **U4,** 40
hear, heard, heard [hɪə, hɜːd, hɜːd] hören **I**
heavy metal [hevi ˈmetl] Heavy Metal **U6,** 58
helicopter [ˈhelɪkɒptə] Hubschrauber **U7,** 67
Hello. [helˈəʊ] Hallo. **I**
say hello [seɪ heˈləʊ] Grüße ausrichten **II**
⟨help⟩ [help] Hilfe **U7,** 75
help [help] helfen **I**
hen [hen] Henne, Huhn **I**
her [hɜː] ihr/ihre **I;** ihr; sie **I**
here [hɪə] hier **I**
Here you are. [hɪə juː ˈɑː] Hier bitte. **I**
herself [həˈself] selbst, sie selbst, sich selbst **U7,** 67
Hey! [heɪ] He! **II**
Hi. [haɪ] Hallo. **I**
high [haɪ] hoch **II**
him [hɪm] ihm; ihn **I**
himself [hɪmˈself] selbst, er selbst, sich selbst **U7,** 70
Hindu [ˈhɪnduː] hinduistisch; Hindu **U1,** 9
his [hɪz] sein/seine **I**
history [ˈhɪstri] Geschichte **U2,** 24
hit [hɪt] Hit **II**
hobby [ˈhɒbi] Hobby **I**
hockey [ˈhɒki] Hockey **I**
⟨hold, held, held⟩ [həʊld, held, held] halten **U3,** 37
⟨hole⟩ [həʊl] Loch **U3,** 37
holiday [ˈhɒlədeɪ] Ferien, Urlaub **I**
home [həʊm] nach Hause **I;** Heim, Zuhause **I**
home game [ˈhəʊm geɪm] Heimspiel **U3,** 33
at home [æt ˈhəʊm] zu Hause; daheim **I**
homework [ˈhəʊmwɜːk] Hausaufgaben **I**
hope [həʊp] hoffen **I**
hot [hɒt] heiß **I**
hotel [həʊˈtel] Hotel **I**
hour [ˈaʊə] Stunde **II**
house [haʊs] Haus **I**
how [haʊ] wie **I**
How are you? [haʊ ˈɑː juː] Wie geht's? **I**
how many [haʊ ˈmeni] wie viele **II**
how much [haʊ ˈmʌtʃ] wie viel **II**
How much are they? [haʊ ˈmʌtʃ ɑː ðeɪ] Wie viel kosten sie? **I**
How much is it? [haʊ ˈmʌtʃ ɪz ɪt] Wie viel kostet es? **I**
How old are you? [haʊ ˈəʊld ɑː juː] Wie alt bist du? **I**
⟨hump⟩ [hʌmp] Höcker **U1,** 19
hundreds [ˈhʌndrədz] hunderte, viele hundert **U1,** 8
hungry [ˈhʌŋgri] hungrig **II**
hurt, hurt, hurt [hɜːt, hɜːt, hɜːt] wehtun, schmerzen **II**

I

I [aɪ] ich **I**
I'd like to …. [aɪd ˈlaɪk tʊ] Ich würde gerne …., Ich möchte …. **I**
I'm …. [aɪm] Ich bin …. **I**

I'm from …. ['aɪm frɒm] Ich komme aus …. **I**
I'm sorry. [aɪm 'sɒri] Tut mir Leid. **I**
ice cream ['aɪs kri:m] Eis, Eiscreme **I**
go **ice skating** [gəʊ 'aɪs skeɪtɪŋ] schlittschuhlaufen gehen **II**
idea [aɪ'dɪə] Idee **I**
ideal [aɪ'dɪəl] ideal **II**
if [ɪf] wenn, falls; ob **U7,** 66
ill [ɪl] krank **II**
important [ɪm'pɔ:tnt] wichtig **II**
in [ɪn] in, im **I**
in English [ɪn 'ɪŋglɪʃ] auf Englisch **U2,** 24
in front of [ɪn 'frʌnt əf] vor **I**
in the evening [ɪn ði: 'i:vnɪŋ] am Abend; abends **I**
in the morning [ɪn ðe 'mɔ:nɪŋ] am Morgen; morgens **I**
in there [ɪn 'ðeə] da drin, dort drin **I**
in town [ɪn 'taʊn] in der Stadt **I**
⟨index finger⟩ ['ɪndeks fɪŋgə] Zeigefinger **U3,** 37
Indian ['ɪndiən] indisch **II**
information [ɪnfə'meɪʃn] Information **I**
Information Centre [ɪnfə'meɪʃn sentə] Informationszentrum **I**
in-line skates ['ɪnlaɪn skeɪts] Inline-Skates, Inliner **I**
instrument ['ɪnstrəmənt] Instrument **U6,** 59
be **interested** in [bɪ: 'ɪntrəstɪd ɪn] interessiert sein an, sich interessieren für **U4,** 39
interesting ['ɪntrəstɪŋ] interessant **I**
internet ['ɪntənet] Internet **II**
on the internet [ɒn ði 'ɪntənet] im Internet **II**
interview ['ɪntəvju:] Interview **U6,** 60
into ['ɪntə] in, hinein **I**
invitation [ɪnvɪ'teɪʃn] Einladung **II**
is [ɪz] ist **I**
How much is it? [haʊ 'mʌtʃ ɪz ɪt] Wie viel kostet es? **I**
… is after you [ɪz 'ɑ:ftə 'ju:] … verfolgt dich, … ist hinter dir her **I**
Is that you? [iz ðæt 'ju:] Bist du es? **U2,** 20
it [ɪt] es **I**
It's …. [ɪts] Es kostet …. **I**
It's a pity [ɪts ə 'pɪti] Es ist schade./Es ist bedauerlich. **U7,** 67
It's Barbara. [ɪts 'bɑ:brɑ] Hier ist Barbara. **U2,** 20
It's me. [ɪts 'mi:] Ich bin's. **U2,** 20

J

January ['dʒænjʊri] Januar **I**
jazz [dʒæz] Jazz **U6,** 58
jealous ['dʒeləs] eifersüchtig **II**
jeans [dʒi:nz] Jeans **II**
jigsaw puzzle ['dʒɪgsɔ: pʌzl] Puzzle **I**
job [dʒɒb] Arbeit, Beruf **I;** Aufgabe **II**
go **jogging** [gəʊ 'dʒɒgɪŋ] joggen gehen **I**
join [dʒɔɪn] beitreten, sich anschließen, verbinden **U8,** 78
joke [dʒəʊk] Witz **I**
journalist ['dʒɜ:nlɪst] Journalist/Journalistin **I**
July [dʒʊ'laɪ] Juli **I**
jump [dʒʌmp] springen **II**
June [dʒu:n] Juni **I**
just [dʒʌst] nur **II;** gerade, soeben **II**
Just a minute, please. [dʒʌzt ə 'mɪnɪt pli:s] Einen Moment bitte. **U5,** 48
Just give it to me. [dʒʌzt 'gɪv ɪt tʊ mi:] Jetzt aber her damit. **II**

K

karaoke [kæri'əʊki] Karaoke **I**
karate [kə'rɑ:ti] Karate **U8,** 76
kebab [kɪ'bæb] Kebab **II**
kick [kɪk] schießen, treten **II**
kilometre [kɪ'lɒmɪtə] Kilometer **II**
king [kɪŋ] König **U1,** 8
kitchen ['kɪtʃɪn] Küche **I**
knife pl. **knives** [naɪf] Messer **I**
know, knew, known [nəʊ, nju:, nəʊn] kennen, wissen **I**
know about [nəʊ ə'baʊt] wissen von **II**

L

lake [leɪk] See **U5,** 46
land [lænd] landen **II**
language ['læŋgwɪdʒ] Sprache **U3,** 26
lantern ['læntən] Laterne **I**
laptop ['læptɒp] Laptop **II**
large [lɑ:dʒ] groß, riesig **I**
last [lɑ:st] letzter/letzte/letztes **II**
last night [lɑ:st 'naɪt] gestern Abend, gestern Nacht **U3,** 28
late [leɪt] spät, zu spät **U1,** 11
Speak to you later. [spi:k tə jə 'leɪtə] Bis später. **U2,** 21
laugh [lɑ:f] lachen **II**
lazy ['leɪzi] faul **I**
learn [lɜ:n] lernen **II**
leave, left, left [li:v, left, left] verlassen, lassen **I;** abfliegen **II**
Leave me alone. [li:v mɪ: ə'ləʊn] Lass mich in Ruhe. **I**
left [left] links **I**
on the left [ɒn ðə 'left] links **I**
leg [leg] Bein **II**
lego ['legəʊ] Lego **I**
leisure centre ['leʒə sentə] Freizeitzentrum **II**
lesson ['lesn] Unterrichtsstunde, Schulstunde **II**
let's [lets] lass/lasst uns **I**
letter ['letə] Buchstabe **I;** Brief **II**
library ['laɪbrəri] Bücherei, Bibliothek **I**
like [laɪk] mögen, gern haben **I**
I'd like to …. [aɪd 'laɪk tʊ] Ich würde gerne …., Ich möchte …. **I**
Would you like … ? [wʊd jə 'laɪk] Möchtest du … ?/ Möchten Sie … ? **I**
like [laɪk] wie **II**
What's … like? ['wɒts 'laɪk] Wie ist … ? **II**
line [laɪn] Linie, Zeile **U1,** 12; Seil, Leine **U7,** 69
link [lɪŋk] Verbindung, Link **II**
list [lɪst] Liste **U1,** 9
listen ['lɪsn] zuhören, anhören **I**
listen to ['lɪsn tʊ] hören, anhören **I**
live [lɪv] wohnen, leben **I**
I lived [lɪvd] ich wohnte/ich habe gewohnt **II**
living room ['lɪvɪŋ ru:m] Wohnzimmer **I**
loch [lɒk] *(das schottische Wort für See)* **U5,** 46
long [lɒŋ] lang **I**
long jump ['lɒŋ dʒʌmp] Weitsprung **I**
look [lʊk] sehen, schauen **I**
good-looking [gʊd 'lʊkɪŋ] gut aussehend **U6,** 60

I've looked at [lʊkt] ich habe angeschaut, ich habe angesehen **II**
look at ['lʊk æt] anschauen, ansehen **I**
look for ['lʊk fɔ:] suchen **I**
lose, **lost**, **lost** [lu:z, lɒst, lɒst] verlieren **U5,** 49
lots of ['lɒts əv] viele **I**
loud [laʊd] laut **II**
loudly ['laʊdli] laut **II**
love [lʌv] Liebe **II**
love [lʌv] lieben, gern mögen **I**
be **lucky** [bi: 'lʌki] Glück haben **I**
lunch [lʌntʃ] Mittagessen **I**
have lunch [hæv 'lʌntʃ] zu Mittag essen **I**
lunch break ['lʌntʃ breɪk] Mittagspause **I**
lyrics ['lɪrɪks] Liedtext **U6,** 60

M

magazine [mægə'zi:n] Zeitschrift, Magazin **U1,** 17
make, **made**, **made** [meɪk, meɪd, meɪd] machen, tun **I**
make up [meɪk 'ʌp] erfinden, sich ausdenken **I**
man pl. **men** [mæn; men] Mann **I**
many ['meni] viele **II**
how many [haʊ 'meni] wie viele **II**
map [mæp] Stadtplan, Landkarte **I**
March [mɑ:tʃ] März **I**
market ['mɑ:kɪt] Markt **I**
marry ['mæri] heiraten **II**
match [mætʃ] zuordnen **U1,** 15
matchstick man ['mætʃstɪk mæn] Strichmännchen **I**
Maths [mæθs] Mathematik **II**
What's the **matter?** [wɒts ðe 'mætə] Was ist los? **II**
may [meɪ] dürfen, können **U1,** 13
May [meɪ] Mai **I**
maybe ['meɪbi] vielleicht **I**
me [mi:] mir; mich **I**; ich **II**
It's me. [ɪts 'mi:] Ich bin's. **U2,** 20
meal [mi:l] Mahlzeit, Essen **I**
mean, **meant**, **meant** [mi:n, ment, ment] bedeuten, heißen **I**
meat [mi:t] Fleisch **II**
mediation [mi:dɪ'eɪʃn] Sprachmittlung **U1,** 15
meet, **met**, **met** [mi:t, met, met] treffen, sich treffen, kennen lernen **I**
Nice to meet you. [naɪs tʊ 'mi:t ju:] Schön dich kennen zu lernen. **I**
meeting place ['mi:tɪŋ pleɪs] Treffpunkt **I**
message ['mesɪdʒ] Mitteilung, Nachricht **II**
metre ['mi:tə] Meter **II**
mice [maɪs] Mäuse **II**
⟨middle⟩ ['mɪdl] Mitte **U3,** 37
milk [mɪlk] Milch **I**
million ['mɪljən] Million **II**
mine [maɪn] Mine **U3,** 29
miner ['maɪnə] Bergarbeiter/Bergarbeiterin **U3,** 29
minute [mɪ'nɪt] Minute **U2,** 20
Just a minute, please. [dʒʌzt ə 'mɪnɪt pli:s] Einen Moment bitte. **U5,** 48
miss [mɪs] vermissen, verpassen, verfehlen **U1,** 10
mobile ['məʊbaɪl] Handy **U2,** 20
mobile phone [məʊbaɪl 'fəʊn] Handy, Mobiltelefon **I**
model ['mɒdl] Modell, Nachbildung **U5,** 51
modern ['mɒdn] modern **I**
Monday ['mʌndeɪ] Montag **I**
money ['mʌni] Geld **I**
monster ['mɒnstə] Monster, Ungeheuer **I**
month [mʌnθ] Monat **I**
more [mɔ:] mehr **II**
more embarrassing [mɔ: ɪm'bærəsɪŋ] peinlicher, unangenehmer **II**
morning ['mɔ:nɪŋ] Morgen, Vormittag **I**
in the morning [ɪn ðe 'mɔ:nɪŋ] am Morgen; morgens **I**
the next morning [ðə nekst 'mɔ:nɪŋ] am nächsten Morgen **U3,** 31
mother ['mʌðə] Mutter **I**
mountain ['maʊntɪn] Berg, Gebirge **U5,** 46
mouse [maʊs] Maus **I**
MP3 player [empi:'θri: pleɪə] MP3 Player **II**
Mr ['mɪstə] *(Anrede)* Herr **I**
Mrs ['mɪsɪz] *(Anrede)* Frau **I**
much [mʌtʃ] viel **I**
how much [haʊ 'mʌtʃ] wie viel **II**
How much are they? [haʊ 'mʌtʃ ɑ: ðeɪ] Wie viel kosten sie? **I**
How much is it? [haʊ 'mʌtʃ ɪz it] Wie viel kostet es? **I**
mum [mʌm] Mama **I**
museum [mju:'zi:əm] Museum **II**
music ['mju:zɪk] Musik **I**
read music [ri:d 'mju:zɪk] Noten lesen **U6,** 59
must [mʌst] müssen **I**
mustn't ['mʌsnt] nicht dürfen **II**
my [maɪ] mein/meine **I**
My name is .... [maɪ 'neɪm ɪz] Ich heiße .... **I**
myself [maɪ'self] selbst, ich selbst, mich selbst **U7,** 67

N

name [neɪm] Name **I**
My name is .... [maɪ 'neɪm ɪz] Ich heiße .... **I**
What's your name? [wɒts jɔ: 'neɪm] Wie heißt du? **I**
⟨nation⟩ ['neɪʃn] Land **U5,** 57
nationality [næʃn'æləti] Staatsangehörigkeit, Nationalität **II**
nature ['neɪtʃə] Natur **U5,** 46
near [nɪə] nahe, in der Nähe von **I**
need [ni:d] brauchen **II**
nervous ['nɜ:vəs] nervös, aufgeregt **II**
network ['netwɜ:k] Netz, Netzwerk **U2,** 20
never ['nevə] nie, niemals **I**
new [nju:] neu **I**
newspaper ['nju:speɪpə] Zeitung ⟨**U5,** 57⟩; **U8,** 77
next [nekst] nächster/nächste/nächstes **II**
next time ['nekst taɪm] nächstes Mal **U4,** 42
next to ['neks tʊ] neben **I**
nice [naɪs] nett, schön **I**
Nice to meet you. [naɪs tʊ 'mi:t ju:] Schön dich kennen zu lernen. **I**
night [naɪt] Nacht **II**
no [nəʊ] kein/keine **II**
no [nəʊ] nein **I**
nobody ['nəʊbədi] niemand, keiner **II**
noise [nɔɪz] Geräusch, Lärm **I**
north [nɔ:θ] Norden **I**
Norwegian [nɔ:'wi:dʒən] Norwegisch **II**
not [nɒt] nicht **I**
not ... any ['nɒt 'eni] kein/keine **II**

not ... anything ['nɒt 'eniθɪŋ] nichts **II**
not yet [nɒt 'jet] noch nicht **U5,** 48
notes [nəʊts] Notizen **U1,** 9
take notes [teɪk 'nəʊts] Notizen machen **U1,** 9
November [nəʊ'vembə] November **I**
now [naʊ] jetzt, nun **I**
number ['nʌmbə] Nummer **I;** Zahl **II**
nurse [nɜːs] Krankenpfleger/Krankenschwester **I**

O

October [ɒk'təʊbə] Oktober **I**
of [ɒv] von **I**
of course [ɒv 'kɔːs] natürlich, selbstverständlich **II**
office ['ɒfɪs] Büro **II**
often ['ɒfn] oft **I**
oh [əʊ] null **I**
Oh. [əʊ] Oh. **I**
OK [əʊ'keɪ] OK, in Ordnung **I**
old [əʊld] alt **I**
How old are you? [haʊ 'əʊld ɑː juː] Wie alt bist du? **I**
on [ɒn] am, auf **I**
on Sunday [ɒn 'sʌndeɪ] am Sonntag; sonntags **I**
on the internet [ɒn ði 'ɪntənet] im Internet **II**
on the programme [ɒn ðə 'prəʊgræm] in der Sendung **I**
on the train [ɒn ðə 'treɪn] im Zug **U1,** 12
once [wans] einmal; einst **U8,** 78
once a week [wʌns ə 'wiːk] einmal pro Woche **U8,** 78
one [wʌn] eins **I;** ein/eine **II**
one hundred [wʌn'hʌndrəd] hundert **II**
one thousand [wʌn 'θauznd] tausend **II**
online [ɒn'laɪn] online **II**
only ['əʊnli] nur **I**
open ['əʊpn] öffnen **I**
open ['əʊpn] offen, geöffnet **I**
opposite ['ɒpəzɪt] gegenüber (von) **I**
or [ɔː] oder **I**
orange juice ['ɒrɪndʒ 'dʒuːs] Orangensaft **I**
orchestra ['ɔːkɪstrə] Orchester **U6,** 59
order ['ɔːdə] Reihenfolge **U1,** 13
order ['ɔːdə] bestellen **U5,** 48
organize ['ɔːgənaɪz] organisieren, koordinieren, veranstalten **U4,** 42
other ['ʌðə] anderer/andere/anderes **I**
ought to ['ɔːt tʊ] sollte/sollten (besser) **U1,** 11
our ['aʊə] unser/unsere **I**
ourselves [aʊə'selvz] selbst, wir selbst, uns selbst **U7,** 70
out of ['aʊt əv] aus ... heraus **II**
outside [aʊt'saɪd] außen, draußen, außerhalb **I**
over ['əʊvə] über **I**
own [əʊn] eigener/eigene/eigenes **I**

P

pack [pæk] einpacken, packen **II**
page [peɪdʒ] Seite **U2,** 20
palace ['pælɪs] Palast **U1,** 8
⟨a sheet of paper⟩ [ə ʃiːt əv 'peɪpə] ein Stück Papier **U3,** 37
parents ['peərənts] Eltern **I**
park [pɑːk] Park **I**
part [pɑːt] Teil **I**
partner ['pɑːtnə] Partner/Partnerin **I**
party ['pɑːti] Party **I**
have a party [hæv ə 'pɑːti] eine Party feiern, eine Party machen **I**
past [pɑːst] nach **I**
half past [hɑːf 'pɑːst] halb **I**
quarter past ['kwɔːtə pɑːst] viertel nach **I**
pasta ['pæstə] Teigwaren, Nudeln **II**
path [pɑːθ] Pfad, Weg **I**
pay, paid, paid [peɪ, peid, peid] zahlen, bezahlen **U2,** 20
PE [piː 'iː] Sportunterricht **II**
pea [piː] Erbse **II**
pen [pen] Füller **I**
pencil ['pentsl] Bleistift **I**
pencil case ['pentsl keɪs] Federmäppchen **I**
penny pl. **pence** ['peni, piː] Pence *(britische Währungseinheit)* **U2,** 20
people ['piːpl] Leute, Menschen **I**
per [pɜː] pro **U2,** 20
⟨period of time⟩ [pɪəriəd əv 'taɪm] Zeitraum **U7,** 75
person ['pɜːsn] Person **U5,** 47
pet [pet] Haustier **I**
phone [fəʊn] Telefon **U1,** 12
phone box ['fəʊn bɒks] Telefonzelle **U2,** 21
phone call ['fəʊn kɔːl] Telefongespräch, Anruf **U2,** 20
phone [fəʊn] anrufen **I**
photo ['fəʊtəʊ] Foto, Fotografie **I**
picture ['pɪktʃə] Bild **I**
take a picture [teɪk ə 'pɪktʃə] fotografieren, ein Foto machen **II**
pig [pɪg] Schwein **I**
⟨pillowcase⟩ ['pɪləʊkeɪs] Kissenbezug **U5,** 57
pilot ['paɪlət] Pilot/Pilotin **U7,** 67
pink [pɪŋk] pink, rosa **I**
pit [pɪt] Grube, Mine **U3,** 29
It's a **pity.** [ɪts ə 'pɪti] Es ist schade./Es ist bedauerlich. **U7,** 67
pizza ['piːtsə] Pizza **II**
place [pleɪs] Ort, Platz, Stelle **II**
plan [plæn] Plan **I;** Programm **U2,** 20
plan [plæn] planen **U4,** 42
plane [pleɪn] Flugzeug **II**
play [pleɪ] Spiel, Theaterstück **I**
play [pleɪ] spielen **I**
play a trick on somebody [pleɪ ə 'trɪk ɒn 'sʌmbədi] jemand einen Streich spielen **II**
player ['pleɪə] Spieler/Spielerin **I**
⟨pleasant⟩ ['pleznt] angenehm **U7,** 75
please [pliːz] bitte **I**
pocket ['pɒkɪt] Hosentasche, Jackentasche **II**
point [pɔɪnt] Punkt **U3,** 33
police pl. **police** [pə'liːs] Polizei **I**
police officer [pə'liːs 'ɒfɪsə] Polizist/Polizistin **I**
pond [pɒnd] Teich **I**
pony ['pəʊni] Pony **I**
pop concert ['pɒp kɒnsət] Popkonzert **II**
pop star ['pɒp stɑː] Popstar **I**
popular ['pɒpjələ] populär, beliebt **U6,** 60
position [pə'zɪʃn] Platz, Position **U3,** 33
post office ['pəʊst ɒfɪs] Postamt **I**
postcard ['pəʊstkɑːd] Postkarte, Ansichtskarte **II**
poster ['pəʊstə] Poster **I**
potato [pə'teɪtəʊ] Kartoffel **II**
pound [paʊnd] Pfund *(britische Währungseinheit)* **I**

practise ['præktɪs] üben **I**
prefer [prɪ'fɜ:] vorziehen, bevorzugen **U8,** 76
present ['preznt] Geschenk **I**
present [prɪ'zent] präsentieren, vorstellen **U4,** 42
presentation [prezn'teɪʃn] Präsentation **U2,** 24
pretty ['prɪti] hübsch **II**
princess [prɪn'ses] Prinzessin **II**
print out [prɪnt 'aʊt] ausdrucken **II**
⟨prison⟩ ['prɪzn] Gefängnis **U5,** 57
private ['praɪvɪt] privat **II**
prize [praɪz] Preis, Gewinn **I**
probably ['prɒbəbli] wahrscheinlich **II**
problem ['prɒblem] Problem **I**
procession [prə'seʃn] Umzug, Festzug **I**
profile ['prəʊfaɪl] *(Zeugnis mit Selbstbeurteilung)* **U4,** 39; Porträt, Profil **U6,** 62
programme ['prəʊgræm] Sendung **I**
on the programme [ɒn ðə 'prəʊgræm] in der Sendung **I**
project ['prɒdʒekt] Projekt **I**
project day ['prɒdʒekt deɪ] Projekttag **I**
⟨protect⟩ [prə'tekt] schützen **U1,** 19; **U7,** 75
pull [pʊl] ziehen **U7,** 67
⟨pull apart⟩ [pʊl ə'pɑ:t] auseinander ziehen **U3,** 37
pupil ['pju:pl] Schüler/Schülerin **I**
push [pʊʃ] stoßen, schieben **II**
put, put, put [pʊt, pʊt, pʊt] setzen, stellen, legen **I;** hineintun, stecken **II;** laden **II**
puzzle ['pʌzl] Rätsel **U1,** 17

Q

quarter past ['kwɔ:tə pɑ:st] viertel nach **I**
queen [kwi:n] Königin **U1,** 8
question ['kwestʃən] Frage **I**
questionnaire [kwestʃə'neə] Fragebogen **U6,** 59
quick [kwɪk] schnell **I**
quiet ['kwaɪət] leise **I**
Be quiet. [bi: 'kwaɪət] Sei/Seid leise. **I**
quite [kwaɪt] ziemlich, ganz **U4,** 39
quiz [kwɪz] Quiz **I**

R

rabbit ['ræbɪt] Kaninchen **I**
race [reɪs] Rennen **I**
radio ['reɪdiəʊ] Radio **I**
rain [reɪn] Regen **U7,** 65
rain [reɪn] regnen **U5,** 46
rainy ['reɪni] regnerisch, verregnet **I**
⟨raise⟩ [reɪz] anheben **U5,** 57
read, read, read [ri:d, red, red] lesen **I**
read music [ri:d 'mju:zɪk] Noten lesen **U6,** 59
ready ['redi] fertig **I**
⟨realize⟩ ['rɪəlaɪz] bemerken **U5,** 57
really ['rɪəli] wirklich **I**
⟨reception⟩ [rɪ'sepʃn] Empfang, Rezeption **U2,** 25
⟨recognize⟩ ['rekəgnaɪz] erkennen **U5,** 57
recorder [rɪ'kɔ:də] Blockflöte **U6,** 59
red [red] rot **I**
registration [redʒɪ'streɪʃn] Anwesenheitskontrolle **II**
relax [rɪ'læks] entspannen, sich beruhigen **II**
remember [rɪ'membə] denken an, sich erinnern **II**
remind somebody [rɪ'maɪnd sʌmbədi] jemanden erinnern **U6,** 59
remote control [rɪməʊt kən'trəʊl] Fernsteuerung, Fernbedienung **U5,** 51
repair [rɪ'peə] reparieren **I**
report [rɪ'pɔ:t] Zeugnis, Bericht **U4,** 39
reporter [rɪ'pɔ:tə] Reporter/Reporterin **I**
restaurant ['restrɑ:ŋ] Restaurant, Gaststätte **I**
result [rɪ'zʌlt] Ergebnis, Resultat **I**
rice [raɪs] Reis **II**
ride, rode, ridden [raɪd, rəʊd, 'rɪdn] fahren, reiten **U5,** 46
right [raɪt] richtig **I;** rechts **I**
be right [bi: 'raɪt] Recht haben **II**
on the right [ɒn ðə 'raɪt] rechts **I**
ring, rang, rung [rɪŋ, ræŋ, rʌŋ] klingeln, läuten **II**
ring tone ['rɪŋ təʊn] Klingelton **U2,** 20
river ['rɪvə] Fluss **I**
road [rəʊd] Straße **I**
robot ['rəʊbɒt] Roboter **I**
⟨roll up⟩ [rəʊl 'ʌp] aufrollen **U3,** 37
room [ru:m] Zimmer, Raum **I**
route [ru:t] Strecke, Route **U5,** 46
go **rowing** [gəʊ 'rəʊɪŋ] rudern gehen **II**
rowing club ['rəʊɪŋ klʌb] Ruderclub **II**
rubber ['rʌbə] Radiergummi **I**
rucksack ['rʌksæk] Rucksack **I**
rule [ru:l] Regel **I**
ruler ['ru:lə] Lineal **I**
run, ran, run [rʌn, ræn, rʌn] laufen, rennen **I**
ran away: I ran away [ræn ə'weɪ] ich lief weg/ich bin weggelaufen **II**
ran into: I ran into [ræn 'ɪntə] ich lief in …hinein/ich bin in … hineingelaufen **II**
run from ['rʌn frɒm] weglaufen vor **I**

S

sad [sæd] traurig, schmerzlich **I**
salad ['sæləd] Salat **II**
the **same** [seɪm] derselbe/dieselbe/dasselbe **I**
sanction ['sænkʃn] Sanktion, Strafe **U4,** 40
⟨sand⟩ [sænd] Sand **U1,** 19
⟨sandstorm⟩ ['sændstɔ:m] Sandsturm **U1,** 19
sandwich ['sænwɪdʒ] Sandwich, belegtes Brot **I**
Saturday ['sætədeɪ] Samstag **I**
save [seɪv] retten **U7,** 67
say, said, said [seɪ, sed, sed] sagen **I**
say hello [seɪ he'ləʊ] Grüße ausrichten **II**
be **scared** [bi: 'skeəd] Angst haben, verängstigt sein **II**
school [sku:l] Schule **I**
school team [sku:l 'ti:m] Schulmannschaft **I**
Science ['saɪəns] Naturwissenschaft, Wissenschaft **II**
Scottish ['skɒtɪʃ] schottisch **U5,** 46
scream [skri:m] schreien **II**
sea [si:] Meer **II**
secret ['si:krət] Geheimnis **II**
security guard [se'kjʊərəti gɑ:d] Wachmann/Wachfrau **II**
see, saw, seen [si:, sɔ:, si:n] sehen **I**
See you there. [si: jə 'ðeə] Wir sehen uns dort. **I**

sell, **sold**, **sold** [sel, səʊld, səʊld] verkaufen **I**
send, **sent**, **sent** [send, sent, sent] schicken, senden **I**
sentence ['sentəns] Satz **U1,** 11
September [sep'tembə] September **I**
she [ʃiː] sie **I**
shed [ʃed] Schuppen **I**
sheep pl. **sheep** [ʃiːp] Schaf **I**
⟨a sheet of paper⟩ [ə ʃiːt əv 'peɪpə] ein Stück Papier **U3,** 37
ship [ʃɪp] Schiff **II**
shirt [ʃɜːt] Hemd **II**
shocked [ʃɒkt] schockiert, erschüttert **U6,** 60
shoe [ʃuː] Schuh **I**
shop [ʃɒp] Laden, Geschäft **I**
go **shopping** [gəʊ 'ʃɒpɪŋ] einkaufen gehen **II**
short [ʃɔːt] kurz **II**
should [ʃʊd] sollte/sollten **II**
you should [ju 'ʃʊd] du solltest **II**
shout [ʃaʊt] schreien, rufen **II**
shout at [ʃaʊt 'æt] anschreien **II**
show [ʃəʊ] zeigen **I**
sight [saɪt] Sehenswürdigkeit **U1,** 8
sign [saɪn] Schild, Zeichen **U7,** 71
simulator ['sɪmjəleɪtə] Simulator **II**
sing, **sang**, **sung** [sɪŋ, sæŋ, sʌŋ] singen **I**
singer ['sɪŋə] Sänger/Sängerin **II**
⟨sink into⟩ [sɪŋk 'ɪntə] einsinken **U1,** 19
sister ['sɪstə] Schwester **I**
sit, **sat**, **sat** [sɪt, sæt, sæt] sitzen **I**
sat down: I sat down [sæt 'daʊn] ich setzte mich hin/ ich habe mich hingesetzt **II**
situation [sɪtju'eɪʃn] Situation, Lage **U4,** 41
skateboard ['skeɪtbɔːd] Skateboard **I**
ski [skiː] Ski **II**
ski jump ['skiː dʒʌmp] Sprungschanze **II**
skirt [skɜːt] Rock **I**
sleep, **slept**, **slept** [sliːp, slept, slept] schlafen **I**
sleeping bag ['sliːpɪŋ bæg] Schlafsack **I**
slow [sləʊ] langsam **II**
slowly ['sləʊli] langsam **II**
small [smɔːl] klein **I**
smelly ['smeli] stinkend **II**
snack [snæk] Imbiss, Snack **I**
snow [snəʊ] Schnee **U7,** 64
so [səʊ] so **I**
so [səʊ] also, folglich **I;** deshalb, daher **II**
sofa ['səʊfə] Sofa **I**
⟨soft⟩ [sɒft] weich **U1,** 19
some [sʌm] einige, etwas **I;** ein paar **II**
somebody ['sʌmbədi] jemand **II**
something ['sʌmθɪŋ] etwas **II**
sometimes ['sʌmtaɪmz] manchmal **I**
son [sʌn] Sohn **II**
song [sɒŋ] Lied **I**
soon [suːn] bald **I**
I'm **sorry.** [aɪm 'sɒri] Tut mir Leid. **I**
sound [saʊnd] Laut, Ton **U5,** 55
south [saʊθ] Süden **I**
southwest [saʊθ'west] südwestlich, Südwest- **I**
speak, **spoke**, **spoken** [spiːk, spəʊk, 'spəʊkn] sprechen **I**
Speak to you later. [spiːk tə jə 'leɪtə] Bis dann. **U2,** 21
This is ... speaking. ['ðɪs ɪz ... 'spiːkɪŋ] Hier spricht ... ., Hier ist ... . **II**
speaker ['spiːkə] Sprecher **U7,** 70
special ['speʃl] besonderer/ besondere/besonderes **I**
spectator [spek'teɪtə] Zuschauer/Zuschauerin **U8,** 76
spectator sport [spek'teɪtə spɔːt] Publikumssport **U8,** 76
spelling ['spelɪŋ] Rechtschreibung **U5,** 55
spicy ['spaɪsi] scharf, stark gewürzt **II**
spider ['spaɪdə] Spinne **I**
split, **split**, **split** [splɪt, splɪt, splɪt] sich trennen **U6,** 60
sponge [spʌndʒ] Schwamm **I**
spoon [spuːn] Löffel **II**
sports [spɔːts] Sport **I**
do sports [duː 'spɔːts] Sport (-arten) treiben **I**
sports field ['spɔːts fiːld] Sportplatz **I**
sports hall ['spɔːts hɔːl] Turnhalle **I**
spring [sprɪŋ] Frühling **I**
stairs [steəz] Treppe **II**
stall [stɔːl] Bude, Stand **I**
stand, **stood**, **stood** [stænd, stʊd, stʊd] stehen **I**
star [stɑː] Star, Stern **I**
start [stɑːt] anfangen **I**
station ['steɪʃn] Haltestelle, Bahnhof **U1,** 12
⟨stay⟩ [steɪ] Aufenthalt **U7,** 75
stay [steɪ] wohnen, übernachten **I;** bleiben **II**
steal, **stole**, **stolen** [stiːl, stəʊl, 'stəʊlən] stehlen **U2,** 22
step [step] Schritt **U8,** 80
still [stɪl] noch **I**
stop [stɒp] aufhören **II**
storm [stɔːm] Sturm **U7,** 65
story ['stɔːri] Geschichte **II**
straight on [streɪt 'ɒn] geradeaus **I**
strange [streɪndʒ] seltsam, sonderbar, merkwürdig **II**
strategy ['strætədʒi] Strategie, Lerntechnik **U2,** 25
street [striːt] Straße **I**
stress [stres] Stress, Belastung **I**
stressed [strest] gestresst, belastet **I**
strict [strɪkt] streng **II**
style [staɪl] Stil, Art **II**
subject ['sʌbdʒɪkt] Schulfach **II**
⟨such⟩ [sʌtʃ] so **U1,** 19
suddenly ['sʌdnli] plötzlich **II**
sugar ['ʃugə] Zucker **II**
summer ['sʌmə] Sommer **I**
Sunday ['sʌndeɪ] Sonntag **I**
on Sunday [ɒn 'sʌndeɪ] am Sonntag; sonntags **I**
sunny ['sʌni] sonnig, heiter **I**
sure [ʃɔː] sicher **I**
surf [sɜːf] surfen **II**
surfing ['sɜːfɪŋ] Surfen **II**
go surfing [gəʊ 'sɜːfɪŋ] surfen gehen **II**
survey ['sɜːveɪ] Umfrage **I**
sweatshirt ['swetʃɜːt] Sweatshirt **I**
swim, **swam**, **swum** [swɪm, swæm, swʌm] schwimmen **U2,** 23
swimmer ['swɪmə] Schwimmer/Schwimmerin **II**
go **swimming** [gəʊ 'swɪmɪŋ] schwimmen gehen **I**
swimming pool ['swɪmɪŋ puːl] Schwimmbad **I**
switch off [swɪtʃ 'ɒf] ausschalten **U2,** 22

T

table ['teɪbl] Tisch **I**
take, **took**, **taken** [teɪk, tʊk, 'teɪkn] nehmen, mitnehmen **I;** nehmen, mit ... fahren **I;** abholen **II;** bringen **II**

take a picture [teɪk ə 'pɪktʃə] fotografieren, ein Foto machen **II**
take notes [teɪk 'nəʊts] Notizen machen **U1,** 9
take part in [teɪk 'pɑ:t ɪn] teilnehmen an **I**
take the times [teɪk ðə 'taɪmz] die Zeiten messen **I**
takeaway ['teɪkəweɪ] Mitnahmerestaurant, Essen zum Mitnehmen **II**
talk [tɔ:k] sprechen, reden **II**
talk about [tɔ:k ə'baʊt] sprechen über, reden über **I**
talk to ['tɔ:k tʊ] sprechen mit, reden mit **I**
tall [tɔ:l] groß, hoch **II**
taxi ['tæksi] Taxi **I**
tea [ti:] Tee **I**
teach, taught, taught [ti:tʃ, tɔ:t, tɔ:t] unterrichten **I**
teacher ['ti:tʃə] Lehrer/Lehrerin **I**
team [ti:m] Mannschaft, Team **I**
⟨teenager⟩ ['ti:neɪdʒə] Teenager **U2,** 25
telephone ['telɪfəʊn] Telefon **I**
television ['telɪvɪʒn] Fernseher **I**
tell, told, told [tel, təʊld, təʊld] sagen, erzählen **I**
tell about [tel ə'baʊt] erzählen von **II**
temperature ['temprətʃə] Temperatur **U7,** 64
temple ['templ] Tempel **U1,** 9
tennis ['tenɪs] Tennis **I**
tent [tent] Zelt **I**
term [tɜ:m] Trimester, Semester **I**
test [test] Test, Klassenarbeit **II**
text [tekst] Text **I**
text message ['tekst 'mesɪdʒ] SMS **II**
text [tekst] eine SMS schreiben **U2,** 20
Text me back. [tekst mi: 'bæk] Schreib zurück (SZ). **II**
than [ðæn] als **II**
thank you ['θæŋkju:] danke (schön) **I**
Fine, thanks. ['faɪn θæŋks] Danke, gut. **I**
that [ðæt] dass **II**
that [ðæt] das; jener/jene/jenes **I**
That's that! [ðæts 'ðæt] Damit basta! **I**
that [ðæt] der/die/das; dem/den *(Relativpronomen)* **U6,** 58
the [ðə, ði:] der/die/das **I**
the most embarrassing [ðə məʊst ɪm'bærəsɪŋ] der/die/das peinlichste, der/die/das unangenehmste **II**
the next morning [ðə nekst 'mɔ:nɪŋ] am nächsten Morgen **U3,** 31
the same [seɪm] derselbe/dieselbe/dasselbe **I**
their [ðeə] ihr/ihre **I**
them [ðem] sie; ihnen **I**
themselves [ðem'selvz] selbst, sie selbst, sich selbst **U7,** 67
then [ðen] dann **I**
there [ðeə] da, dort **I;** da hin, dort hin **II**
in there [ɪn 'ðeə] da drin, dort drin **I**
See you there. [si: jə 'ðeə] Wir sehen uns dort. **I**
there are [ðeə 'ɑ:] da sind **I**
there is [ðeə 'ɪz] da ist, es gibt, es ist **I**
these [ði:z] diese **I**
they [ðeɪ] *(pl.)* sie **I**
They're .... [ðeə] Sie kosten .... **I**
thing [θɪŋ] Ding, Sache **I**
think, thought, thought [θɪŋk, θɔ:t, θɔ:t] finden, meinen, denken **I**
thirsty ['θɜ:sti] durstig **I**
this [ðɪs] dieser/diese/dieses **I**
this is ['ðɪs ɪz] dies ist, das ist **I**
This is ... speaking. ['ðɪs ɪz ... 'spi:kɪŋ] Hier spricht ... ., Hier ist .... **II**
this is why [ðɪs ɪz 'waɪ] deshalb **I**
this afternoon [ðɪs ɑ:ftə'nu:n] heute Nachmittag **U3,** 28
those [ðəʊz] jene **I**
thousands ['θaʊzəndz] tausende, viele tausend **U7,** 64
through [θru:] durch **U5,** 51
throw, threw, thrown [θrəʊ, θru:, θrəʊn] werfen **I**
Thursday ['θɜ:zdeɪ] Donnerstag **I**
ticket ['tɪkɪt] Eintrittskarte, Ticket **I**
tidy up [taɪdi 'ʌp] aufräumen **II**
tidy ['taɪdi] ordentlich **I**
time [taɪm] Zeit **I**
next time ['nekst taɪm] nächstes Mal **U4,** 42
take the times [teɪk ðə 'taɪmz] die Zeiten messen **I**
What time is it? [wɒt 'taɪm ɪz ɪt] Wie viel Uhr ist es? **I**
timetable ['taɪmteɪbl] Stundenplan **II**
tip [tɪp] Ratschlag, Tipp **U1,** 15; Spitze ⟨**U3,** 37⟩
tired ['taɪəd] müde **I**
title ['taɪtl] Titel, Überschrift **U6,** 60
to [tʊ] vor **I;** an, nach, zu **I**
to [tʊ] um zu **I**
toast [təʊst] Toast(brot) **I**
today [tə'deɪ] heute **I**
together [tə'geðə] zusammen **II**
toilet ['tɔɪlət] Toilette **I**
tomorrow [tə'mɒrəʊ] morgen **I**
⟨ton⟩ [tʌn] Tonne **U7,** 75
tonight [tə'naɪt] heute Abend, heute Nacht **U3,** 29
too [tu:] auch **I;** zu **I**
top [tɒp] oberer Teil, Spitze **II**
topic ['tɒpɪk] Thema **U2,** 20
torch [tɔ:tʃ] Taschenlampe **I**
tornado [tɔ:'neɪdəʊ] Tornado **U7,** 65
totally ['təʊtəli] total, völlig **U6,** 58
tour [tʊə] Führung, Tour **U3,** 32
tourist ['tʊərɪst] Tourist/Touristin **I**
⟨towel⟩ [taʊəl] Handtuch **U7,** 75
⟨towel rack⟩ [taʊəl 'ræk] Handtuchhalter **U7,** 75
tower ['taʊə] Turm **II**
town [taʊn] Stadt **I**
in town [ɪn 'taʊn] in der Stadt **I**
town centre [taʊn 'sentə] Stadtzentrum **U7,** 65
tractor ['træktə] Traktor **I**
train [treɪn] Zug **I**
on the train [ɒn ðə 'treɪn] im Zug **U1,** 12
train [treɪn] trainieren **I**
trainer ['treɪnə] Turnschuh **II**
training ['treɪnɪŋ] Training **U3,** 28
tree [tri:] Baum **I**
trick [trɪk] Trick **I**
play a trick on somebody [pleɪ ə 'trɪk ɒn 'sʌmbədi] jemand einen Streich spielen **II**
trip [trɪp] Fahrt, Reise **U1,** 14
camping trip ['kæmpɪŋ trɪp] Campingausflug, Campingtrip **II**

go on a trip [gəʊ ɒn ə 'trɪp] einen Ausflug machen, eine Reise machen **II**
trombone [trɒm'bəʊn] Posaune **U3, 26**
trouble ['trʌbl] Schwierigkeiten, Ärger **I**
trousers ['traʊzez] Hose **I**
true [tru:] wahr **II**
trumpet ['trʌmpɪt] Trompete **U6, 59**
try [traɪ] versuchen, ausprobieren **I**
T-shirt ['ti:ʃɜ:t] T-Shirt **I**
Tuesday ['tju:zdeɪ] Dienstag **I**
tunnel ['tʌnl] Tunnel, Unterführung **I**
turn [tɜ:n] abbiegen **I**
tutor group ['tju:tə gru:p] Klasse *(in einer englischen Schule)* **I**
TV [ti:'vi:] Fernseher **I**
twenty-six [twenti 'sɪks] sechsundzwanzig **I**
⟨twice⟩ [twaɪs] zweimal **U7, 75**
twinned [twɪnd] verschwistert **U3, 26**
type [taɪp] Typ **U8, 78**
type in [taɪp 'ɪn] eingeben **II**

U

uncle ['ʌŋkl] Onkel **U1, 8**
under ['ʌndə] unter **I**
Underground ['ʌndəgraʊnd] U-Bahn **I**
understand, understood, understood [ʌndə'stænd, ʌndə'stʊd, ʌndə'stʊd] verstehen **II**
unhappy [ʌn'hæpi] unglücklich **U6, 60**
uniform ['ju:nɪfɔ:m] Uniform **I**
unit ['ju:nɪt] Kapitel **U1, 15**
until [ʌn'tɪl] bis **II**
up [ʌp] hoch, hinauf **II**
upset [ʌp'set] bestürzt, aufgeregt **II**
us [ʌs] uns; wir **I**
use [ju:z] benutzen, verwenden **II**
⟨by using …⟩ [baɪ 'ju:zɪŋ] indem Sie … benutzen **U7, 75**
usually ['ju:ʒli] normalerweise, gewöhnlich **I**

V

valley ['væli] Tal **U7, 66**
van [væn] Lieferwagen, Kleintransporter **I**
vegetable ['vedʒtəbl] Gemüse **I**
vegetarian [vedʒɪ'teəriən] Vegetarier/Vegetarierin **II**
vegetarian [vedʒɪ'teəriən] vegetarisch **II**
very ['veri] sehr **I**
video camera ['vɪdiəʊ kæmrə] Videokamera, Camcorder **I**
Viking ['vaɪkɪŋ] Wikinger **II**
village ['vɪlɪdʒ] Dorf **II**
visit ['vɪzɪt] Besuch **I**
visit ['vɪzɪt] besuchen **I**; besichtigen **II**
voice [vɔɪs] Stimme **II**
volleyball ['vɒlibɔ:l] Volleyball **I**

W

wait [weɪt] warten **I**
wait for [weɪt 'fɔ:] warten auf **II**
walk [wɔ:k] gehen, laufen **I**
wall [wɔ:l] Wand ⟨**U3, 37**⟩; **U4, 41**
wallet ['wɒlɪt] Brieftasche **II**
want (to) ['wɒnt tʊ] wollen, mögen **I**
warm [wɔ:m] warm **U7, 64**
wash [wɒʃ] waschen **I**
wash up [wɒʃ 'ʌp] abwaschen, abspülen **II**
⟨waste⟩ [weɪst] verschwenden **U7, 75**
watch [wɒtʃ] Armbanduhr **U3, 30**
watch [wɒtʃ] anschauen, zusehen **I**; beobachten **I**
water ['wɔ:tə] Wasser **I**
way [weɪ] Art, Weg, Methode **U2, 24**
we [wi:] wir **I**
wear, wore, worn *(Kleidung)* [weə, wɔ:, wɔ:n] anhaben, tragen **I**
weather ['weðə] Wetter **I**
web [web] Netz, Netzwerk **U1, 16**
website ['websaɪt] Website **II**
wedding ['wedɪŋ] Hochzeit **U1, 9**
Wednesday ['wenzdeɪ] Mittwoch **I**
week [wi:k] Woche **I**
weekend [wi:k'end] Wochenende **I**
at the weekend [æt ðe wi:k'end] am Wochenende **I**
welcome ['welkʌm] willkommen **U3, 26**
You're welcome. [jɔ: 'welkəm] Bitte./Gern geschehen. **I**
well [wel] gut **U3, 30**
well [wel] nun (ja) **II**
Welsh [welʃ] walisisch; Waliser/Waliserin **U3, 26**
west [west] Westen **I**
West Indian [west 'ɪndiən] westindisch; Westinder/Westinderin **U1, 12**
wet [wet] nass **II**
what [wɒt] was **I**; welcher/welche/welches **I**
What colour is … ? [wɒt 'kʌlər ɪz] Welche Farbe hat … ? **I**
What's happening? [wɒts 'hæpenɪŋ] Was geht hier vor? **I**
What's … like? ['wɒts 'laɪk] Wie ist …? **II**
What's missing? [wɒts 'mɪsɪŋ] Was fehlt? **U1, 10**
What's the matter? [wɒts ðe 'mætə] Was ist los? **II**
What's wrong? [wɒts 'rɒŋ] Was ist los? **I**
What's your name? [wɒts jɔ: 'neɪm] Wie heißt du? **I**
⟨What the heck …?⟩ [wɒt ðə 'hek] Was, zum Teufel …? **U1, 19**
What time is it? [wɒt 'taɪm ɪz ɪt] Wie viel Uhr ist es? **I**
when [wen] wenn **II**; als **II**
when [wen] wann **I**
where [weə] wo **I**; wohin **I**
Where are you from? [weər ɑ: jə 'frɒm] Woher kommst du? **I**
which [wɪtʃ] welcher/welche/welches **I**
white [waɪt] weiß **II**
who [hu:] wer **I**
⟨whole⟩ [həʊl] ganz **U5, 57**
why [waɪ] warum **I**
this is why [ðɪs ɪz 'waɪ] deshalb **I**
wide [waɪd] breit **II**
wild [waɪld] wild **I**
will [wɪl] werden **II**
won't [wəʊnt] nicht werden **II**
win, won, won [wɪn, wʌn, wʌn] gewinnen **I**
wind [wɪnd] Wind **U7, 65**
window ['wɪndəʊ] Fenster **I**
winter ['wɪntə] Winter **I**
witch [wɪtʃ] Hexe **U7, 68**
witchcraft ['wɪtʃkrɑ:ft] Hexerei **U7, 66**
with [wɪð] mit, mit … zusammen, bei **I**

without [wɪ'ðaʊt] ohne **II**
woman pl. **women** ['wʊmən; 'wɪmɪn] Frau **I**
word [wɜ:d] Wort **I**
work [wɜ:k] Arbeit **I**
work [wɜ:k] arbeiten **I**; funktionieren **I**
worksheet ['wɜ:kʃi:t] Arbeitsblatt **I**
worried ['wʌrid] beunruhigt, besorgt **I**
worse [wɜ:s] schlechter, schlimmer **II**
the **worst** [wɜ:st] der/die/das schlechteste, der/die/das schlimmste **II**
I'd like to .... [aɪd 'laɪk tʊ] Ich würde gerne ...., Ich möchte .... **I**
Would you like ... ? [wʊd jə 'laɪk] Möchtest du ... ?/ Möchten Sie ... ? **I**
write, wrote, written [raɪt, rəʊt, 'rɪtn] schreiben **I**
wrong [rɒŋ] falsch **I**
be wrong [bi: 'rɒŋ] Unrecht haben **U2,** 23
What's wrong? [wɒts 'rɒŋ] Was ist los? **I**

Y

yeah [jeə] ja **II**
year [jɪə] Jahr **I**
Year 7 [jiə 'sevn] Klasse sieben **I**
yellow ['jeləʊ] gelb **I**
yes [jes] ja **I**
yesterday ['jestədeɪ] gestern **II**
yet [jet] schon, noch **II**
not yet [nɒt 'jet] noch nicht **U5,** 48
yoga ['jəʊgə] Yoga **II**
yoghurt ['jɒgət] Joghurt **II**
you [ju:] du **I**; ihr **I**; dir; dich **I**; euch **I**; man **II**
you should [ju 'ʃʊd] du solltest **II**
You're welcome. [jɔ: 'welkəm] Bitte./Gern geschehen. **I**
young [jʌŋ] jung **I**
⟨youngster⟩ ['jʌŋstə] Jugendliche/Jugendlicher **U1,** 19
your [jɔ:] dein/deine **I**; euer/eure, Ihr/Ihre **I**
yourself [jɔ:'self] selbst, du selbst, dich selbst **U7,** 67
youth hostel ['ju:θ hɒstl] Jugendherberge **U5,** 47

Z

zoo [zu:] Zoo **II**

Boys' names

Alex ['ælɪks] **U6,** 58
Andrew ['ændru:] **U5,** 48
Andy ['ændi] **I**
Ashraf ['æʃrəv] **U8,** 76
Ben [ben] **I**
Brad [bræd] **II**
Charles [tʃɑ:lz] **II**
Dan [dæn] **I**
Fred [fred] **U1,** 10
Jake [dʒeɪk] **II**
Lars [lɑ:z] **II**
Leroy ['li:rɔɪ] **II**
Luke [lu:k] **I**
Mark [mɑ:k] **I**
Matt [mæt] **I**
Max [mæks] ⟨**U4,** 43⟩; **U7,** 71
Peter ['pi:tə] **II**
Rhodri ['rɒdri] **U3,** 27
Richard ['rɪtʃəd] **I**
Sam [sæm] **I**
Scott [skɒt] **I**
Simon ['saɪmən] **I**
Sridhar ['srɪdhɑ:] **II**
Steven ['sti:vn] **I**
Sven [sven] **II**
Terry ['teri] **I**
Tim [tɪm] **I**
Tom [tɒm] **I**
Tommy ['tɒmi] **U6,** 62

Girls' names

Alexandra [ælɪg'zɑ:ndrə] **U4,** 38
Anna ['ænə] **I**
Barbara ['bɑ:brə] **II**
Claire [kleə] **U6,** 58
Eleanor ['elɪnə] **II**
Emma ['emə] **I**
Eva ['ɪ:və] **I**
Farah ['fɑ:rə] **I**
Francesca [fræn'tʃeskə] **U2,** 23
Gemma ['dʒemə] **II**
Helen ['helən] **I**
Jade [dʒeɪd] **I**
Jenny ['dʒeni] **I**
Karita [kʌ'ri:tʌ] **II**
Kate [keɪt] **U7,** 67
Katie ['keɪti] **I**
Kelly ['keli] **U6,** 60
Kerry ['keri] **U3,** 26
Linda ['lɪndə] **I**
Lisa ['li:sə] **I**
Louise [lu'i:z] **U1,** 14
Lucy ['lu:si] **U5,** 53
Margaret ['mɑ:grət] **II**
Meg [meg] **II**
Naomi ['neɪəmi] **U4,** 42
Nasreen [nʌs'ri:n] **I**
Nicky ['nɪki] **U8,** 78
Nina ['ni:nə] **I**
Sarah ['seərə] **II**
Sonja ['sɒnjə] **II**
Sue [su:] **U7,** 71
Susan ['su:zn] **I**
Susie ['su:zi] **I**
Tammy ['tæmi] **U5,** 52
Tara ['tɑ:rə] **I**
Ulrika [ʊl'ri:kʌ] **II**

Surnames

Baker ['beɪkə] **II**
Barnes [bɑ:nz] **U4,** 39
Beckham ['bekəm] **II**
Benson ['bensn] **U7,** 68
Bray [breɪ] **I**
Brook [brʊk] **I**
Brown [braʊn] **I**
Burns [bɜ:nz] **U5,** 45
Carter ['kɑ:tə] **I**
Clark [klɑ:k] **I**
Cook [kʊk] **II**
Harvey ['hɑ:vi] **I**
Hu [hu:] **I**
Jackson ['dʒæksən] **I**
Jones [dʒəʊnz] **U3,** 27
McWilliams [mək'wɪljəmz] **U5,** 48
Newman ['nju:mən] **I**
Olsen ['əʊlsən] **II**
Penford ['penfɔ:d] **I**
Richards ['rɪtʃədz] **I**
Rose [rəʊz] **I**
Spencer ['spentsə] **I**
Stone [stəʊn] **II**
Taylor ['teɪlə] **I**
Uddin ['ʌdɪn] **II**
Webb [web] **I**
⟨Wilder⟩ ['waɪldə] **U5,** 57
Williams ['wɪljəmz] **I**

Place names

Abergavenny [æbəgə'veni] **U3,** 26
America [ə'merɪkə] **U1,** 8
⟨Arkansas⟩ ['ɑ:kənsɔ:] **U5,** 57
Australia [ɒs'treɪliə] **II**
Baker Street ['beɪkə stri:t] **U1,** 15
Ben Nevis [ben 'nevɪs] **U5,** 46
Berlin [bɜ:'lɪn] **I**
Birmingham ['bɜ:mɪŋəm] **U6,** 60

Boscastle ['bɒskɑ:sl] **U7,** 66
Bristol ['brɪstl] **U6,** 60
Cardiff ['kɑ:dɪf] **U6,** 60
Carmarthen [kə'mɑ:ðən] **U3,** 30
Cornwall ['kɔ:nwɔ:l] **U7,** 66
Crane Street ['kreɪn stri:t] **I**
Dartmoor ['dɑ:tmɔ:] **I**
Devon ['devn] **I**
Dorset ['dɔ:sɪt] **II**
Edinburgh ['edɪnbrə] **U5,** 46
England ['ɪŋglənd] **I**
Europe ['jʊərəp] **U1,** 9
Germany ['dʒɜ:məni] **I**
Greenwich ['grenɪdʒ] **I**
Greenwich Market [grenɪdʒ 'mɑ:kɪt] **I**
Greenwich Road [grenɪdʒ 'rəʊd] **I**
Hither Farm Road [hɪðə fɑ:m 'rəʊd] **I**
Holburn Road [hɒlbɜ:n 'rəʊd] **I**
India ['ɪndiə] **I**
Italy ['ɪtli] **II**
King William Walk [kɪŋ wɪljəm 'wɒ:k] **I**
Loch Ness [lɒk 'nes] **U5,** 46
London ['lʌndən] **I**
London Road [lʌndən 'rəʊd] **I**
Manchester ['mæntʃɪstə] **U8,** 76
Mars [mɑ:z] **II**
Monmouth Town [mɒnməθ 'taʊn] **U3,** 32
Nelson Road [nelsn 'rəʊd] **I**
Newtown ['nju:taʊn] **U3,** 32
New York [nju:'jɔ:k] **I**
Norway ['nɔ:weɪ] **II**
Oslo ['ɒzləʊ] **II**
Oxford Street ['ɒksfəd stri:t] **II**
Park Row [pɑ:k 'rəʊ] **I**
Piccadilly Circus [pɪkədɪli 'sɜ:kəs] **U1,** 13
River Thames [rɪvə 'temz] **I**
Rogestone ['rɒdʒəstən] **U3,** 32
Romney Road [rɒmni 'rəʊd] **I**
Scotland ['skɒtlənd] **U5,** 46
Stonehenge [stəʊn'hendʒ] **II**
Trafalgar Square [trəfælgə 'skweə] **U1,** 13
Turkey ['tɜ:ki] **II**
UK (United Kingdom) [ju:'keɪ, ju:naɪtɪd 'kɪŋdəm] **U2,** 20
Wales [weɪlz] **U3,** 26
Wendover Road [wendəʊvə 'rəʊd] **I**
West End [west 'end] **U1,** 9

Other names

A. C. Pontymiste [eɪsi: pɒntɪ'mɪst] **U3,** 32
Bakerloo Line ['beɪkəlu: laɪn] **U1,** 15
Barker ['bɑ:kə] **I**
Beatles ['bi:tlz] **I**
Big Ben [bɪg 'ben] **U1,** 15
Big Pit [bɪg 'pɪt] **U3,** 29
Blue Note Café [blu: nəʊt 'kæfeɪ] **I**
Brad Pitt [bræd 'pɪt] **I**
Britney Spears [brɪtni 'spɪəz] **II**
Buckingham Palace [bʌkɪŋəm 'pælɪs] **U1,** 8
Bugsy Malone [bʌgzi mə'ləʊn] **I**
Burger Bar ['bɜ:gə bɑ:] **I**
Café Mambo [kæfeɪ 'mæmbəʊ] **U1,** 13
Canary Wharf tower [kəneəri wɔ:f 'taʊə] **II**
Carmarthen Castle [kəmɑ:θən 'kɑ:sl] **U3,** 30
Central Line ['sentrl laɪn] **U1,** 12
Charing Cross [tʃærɪŋ 'krɒs] **U1,** 15
Chicago Bulls [ʃɪkɑ:gəʊ 'bʊlz] **II**
Childline ['tʃaɪldlaɪn] **U4,** 42
Circle Line ['sɜ:kl laɪn] **U1,** 15
Cutty Sark [kʌti 'sɑ:k] **I**
Dartmoor Safaris [dɑ:tmɔ: sə'fɑ:riz] **I**
David Bowie [deɪvɪd 'baʊi] **I**
Eastlife ['i:stlaɪf] **II**
Formula One [fɔ:mjələ 'wʌn] **I**
Galaxy Radio [gæləksi 'reɪdiəʊ] **I**
Garden Restaurant [gɑ:dn 'restrɑ:ŋ] **I**
Greendale Farm [gri:ndeɪl 'fɑ:m] **I**
Greenwich Mean Time [grenɪdʒ 'mi:n taɪm] **I**
Javine [dʒə'vi:n] **U6,** 58
Kensington ['kenzɪŋgtən] **U1,** 15
London Eye [lʌndən 'aɪ] **U1,** 10
London Marathon [lʌndən 'mærəθn] **II**
Manchester United [mæntʃɪstə ju:'naɪtɪd] **U3,** 27
Matrix ['meɪtrɪks] **U6,** 60
McFly [mək'flaɪ] **U6,** 60
Meridian Line [mə'rɪdiən laɪn] **I**
Millennium Dome [mɪleniəm 'dəʊm] **II**
Mr Bean [mɪstə 'bi:n] **I**
Nessie ['nesi] **U5,** 46
Notting Hill Carnival [nɒtɪŋ hɪl 'kɑ:nɪvl] **U1,** 8
Notting Hill Gate [nɒtɪŋ hɪl 'geit] **U1,** 12
Oban Hostel [əʊbn 'hɒstl] **U5,** 47
Oxford Circus ['ɒksfəd sɜ:kəs] **U1,** 12
oznet.au [ɒznet'ɒ] **II**
Paddington Station [pædɪŋtən 'steɪʃn] **U1,** 15
Riverford Farm [rɪvəfɔ:d 'fɑ:m] **I**
Robbie Williams [rɒbi 'wɪljəmz] **I**
Royal Observatory [rɔɪəl əb'zɜ:vətri] **I**
St Paul's Cathedral [snt'pɔ:lz kə'θi:drl] **II**
Superman ['su:pəmæn] **U5,** 48
telnet.uk ['telnet ju:'keɪ] **II**
Thomas Tallis School [tɒməs tælɪs 'sku:l] **I**
Tillery United [tɪləri ju:'naɪtid] **U3,** 32
Tower of London [taʊə əv 'lʌndn] **U1,** 8
Venus Williams [vi:nəs 'wɪljəmz] **I**
Waves [weɪvz] **II**
Westlands High School ['westləndz 'haɪ sku:l] **U4,** 38
Westminster [west'mɪntstə] **U1,** 15
Will Young [wɪl 'jʌŋ] **I**
Wimbledon ['wɪmbldn] **I**
With Time [wɪð 'taɪm] **I**
Woodlands ['wʊdləndz] **I**
World Time ['wɜ:ld taɪm] **I**
X-Boys ['eks bɔɪz] **I**

A

abbiegen turn
Abend evening
abends in the evening
am Abend in the evening
den ganzen Abend lang all evening
zu Abend essen have dinner
Abendessen dinner
Abenteuer adventure
aber but
abfliegen leave
Abflug departure
abholen fetch; take
Abreise departure
abspülen wash up
abwaschen wash up
Acker field
addieren add
Adresse address
aktiv active
Aktivität activity
alle all
alleine alone
alles all
Alphabet alphabet
als than; when; as
also so
alt old
Wie alt bist du? How old are you?
am on
am Abend in the evening
am Leben sein be alive
am Morgen in the morning
am nächsten Morgen the next morning
am Sonntag on Sunday
am Wochenende at the weekend
an at; to
anderer/andere/anderes other
anders different
anfangen start
Angst haben be scared
anhaben wear *(Kleidung)*
anhören listen; listen to
anklicken click on
ankommen arrive
Anorak anorak
Anruf phone call
anrufen phone; call
Anrufer/Anruferin caller
anschauen watch; look at
Anschlagtafel board
anschreien shout at
ansehen look at
Ansichtskarte postcard
Antwort answer
antworten answer
Anwesenheitskontrolle registration
Apfel apple
April April
Arbeit job; work
arbeiten work
Arbeitsblatt worksheet
Ärger trouble
Armbanduhr watch
Art style; way
atmen breathe
auch too; also
auf at; on
auf Englisch in English
Auf Wiedersehen. Goodbye.
Aufgabe job
aufgeregt upset; nervous; excited
aufhören finish; stop
aufräumen tidy up
aufstehen get up
Auge eye
August August
aus from
aus ... heraus out of
ausdrucken print out
ausfahren go out
einen **Ausflug machen** go on a trip
ausgehen go out
ausprobieren try
Grüße **ausrichten** say hello
ausschalten switch off
außen outside
außerhalb outside
äußerster/äußerste/äußerstes extreme
aussteigen get off
Ausstellung exhibition
Austausch exchange
Auswärtsspiel away game
Auto car

B

Badezimmer bathroom
Bahnhof station
bald soon
Ball ball
Band band
Basketball basketball
Bauernhof farm
Baum tree
beantworten answer
Es ist **bedauerlich.** It's a pity.
bedeuten mean
beeindruckend awesome
beenden finish
begeistert excited
bei at; with
Bein leg
beinahe almost
beitreten join
bekommen get
belastet stressed
Belastung stress
belegtes Brot sandwich
beliebt popular
bellen bark
benutzen use
beobachten watch
bereits already
Berg mountain
Bergarbeiter/Bergarbeiterin miner
Bericht report
Beruf job
berühmt famous
beschäftigt busy
besichtigen visit
besitzen have got
besonderer/besondere/besonderes special
besorgt worried
besser better
der/die/das beste best
bestellen order
bestürzt upset
Besuch visit
besuchen visit
Bett bed
ins Bett gehen go to bed
beunruhigt worried
bevor before
bevorzugen prefer
bewölkt cloudy
bezahlen pay
Bibliothek library
Bild picture
billig cheap
bis until
Bis dann. Speak to you later.
bist are
Bist du es? Is that you?
Bist du schon einmal in Deutschland gewesen? Have you ever been to Germany?
bitte please; You're welcome.
blau blue
bleiben stay
Bleistift pencil
Blockflöte recorder
blond blonde
Boot boat
Boy Group boy band
braun brown
brechen break
breit wide
Brief letter
Brieftasche wallet
Brille glasses
bringen take
britisch British

Bruder brother
Buch book
buchen book
Bücherei library
Buchstabe letter
Bude stall
Bulle bull
Bungeespringen bungee jumping
Büro office
Bus bus
mit dem Bus by bus
Busch bush
Butter butter

C

Café café
Cafeteria cafeteria
Camcorder video camera
Campingausflug camping trip
Campingplatz campsite
Campingtrip camping trip
Cartoon cartoon
CD CD
Champion champion
Checkliste checklist
chinesisch Chinese
circa about
Clown clown
Club club
Comicheft comic
Computer computer
cool cool
Cornflakes cornflakes
Couchpotato couch potato
Cousin/Cousine cousin
Curry curry
Currygericht curry

D

da there
da drin in there
da hin there
da ist there is
da sind there are
Dachboden attic
daheim at home
daher so
Damit basta! That's that!
danach after that
danke (schön) thank you
Danke, gut. Fine, thanks.
dann then
Darts darts
das the; that
das ist this is
dasselbe the same
dein/deine your
dem that
Demonstration demonstration
den that
denken think; believe
denken an remember
der the; that
derselbe the same
deshalb this is why; so
Detektiv/Detektivin detective
Detektivgeschichte detective story
deutsch German
Deutsch German
Deutscher/Deutsche German
Dezember December
Dialog dialogue
Diät diet
dich you
dich selbst yourself
dick big
die the; that
Dienstag Tuesday
dieser/diese/dieses this
dies ist this is
diese these
dieselbe the same
Ding thing
dir you
Diskjockey DJ
Disko disco
Diskus discus
diskutieren argue
Donnerstag Thursday
Dorf village
dort there
dort drin in there
dort hin there
drangsalieren bully
draußen outside
du you
du selbst yourself
dunkel dark
durch through
dürfen may
durstig thirsty
DVD DVD
DVD-Spieler DVD player

E

Ei egg
eifersüchtig jealous
eigener/eigene/eigenes own
ein/eine a; an; one
Einen Moment bitte. Just a minute, please.
ein anderer/eine andere/ein anderes another
ein paar some
einatmen breathe in
Einband cover
Einbruch break-in
einfach easy
eingeben type in
einige some
einkaufen gehen go shopping
Einladung invitation
einmal once
einmal pro Woche once a week
einpacken pack
einst once
Eintrittskarte ticket
Eis ice cream
Eiscreme ice cream
Eltern parents
E-Mail e-mail
Ende end; ending
enden finish
Engländer/Engländerin English
Englisch English
auf Englisch in English
Ente duck
entlang along
entscheiden decide
Entschuldigung. Excuse me.
entspannen relax
Entwurf design
er he
er selbst himself
Erbse pea
Erdkunde Geography
Ereignis event
erfahren über find out about
erfinden make up
Ergebnis result
jemanden **erinnern** remind somebody
erschüttert shocked
erzählen tell
erzählen von tell about
es it
Es ist bedauerlich. It's a pity.
es gibt there are; there is
es ist there is
Es ist schade. It's a pity.
Es kostet .... It's ....
es sind there are
essen eat
Essen food; meal
Essen zum Mitnehmen takeaway
Esszimmer dining room
etwas some; something
euch you
euer/eure your
Euro euro
extrem extreme
Extremsport extreme sports

F

fahren go; drive; ride
mit ... fahren take
Fahrer/Fahrerin driver
Fahrrad bike
Fahrt trip
fair fair
fallen fall
falls if
falsch wrong
Familie family
Fan fan
fantastisch fantastic
Farbe colour
Welche Farbe hat ... ? What colour is ... ?
fast almost
faul lazy
Februar February
Federmäppchen pencil case
Was **fehlt?** What's missing?
Feld field
Fenster window
Ferien holiday
Ferienwohnung cottage
Fernbedienung remote control
Fernseher TV; television
Fernsehglotzer/Fernsehglotzerin couch potato
Fernsteuerung remote control
fertig ready
Festzug procession
Film film
Filzstift felt-tip
Finale final
finden find; think
Fisch fish pl. fish
fit fit
Fleisch meat
fliegen fly
Flug flight
Flughafen airport
Flugnummer flight number
Flugsteig gate
Flugzeug plane
Fluss river
folgen follow
folglich so
in **Form** fit
Foto photo
ein Foto machen take a picture
Fotoapparat camera
Fotografie photo
fotografieren take a picture
Frage question
Fragebogen questionnaire
fragen ask
Frau woman pl. women; Mrs *(Anrede)*
Freak freak
frei free
Freitag Friday
Freizeitzentrum activity centre; leisure centre
fressen eat
Freund boyfriend
Freund/Freundin friend
Freundin girlfriend
frisch fresh
froh happy
Frosch frog
Frucht fruit
Frühling spring
Frühstück breakfast
zum Frühstück for breakfast
frühstücken have breakfast
Frühstückspension bed and breakfast (B & B)
fühlen feel
Führung tour
Füller pen
funktionieren work
für for
furchtbar awful
Fußball football
füttern feed

G

Gabel fork
Galaxie galaxy
ganz quite
Garten garden
Gast guest
Gaststätte restaurant
geben give, gave, given
Gebirge mountain
Geburtstag birthday
Herzlichen Glückwunsch zum Geburtstag! Happy birthday!
Gebüsch bush
gefährlich dangerous
gegen against
gegenüber (von) opposite
Geheimnis secret
gehen go; walk
Was geht hier vor? What's happening?
Wie geht's? How are you?
Geist ghost
gelb yellow
Geld money
Gemüse vegetable
genießen enjoy
geöffnet open
Geografie Geography
gerade just
geradeaus straight on
Geräusch noise
gerecht fair
Gern geschehen. You're welcome.
gern haben like
gern mögen love
Geschäft shop
geschehen happen
Geschenk present
Geschichte story; history
geschlossen closed
Gesicht face
Gespräch dialogue
gestern yesterday
gestern Abend last night
gestern Nacht last night
gestresst stressed
Getränk drink
Gewinn prize
gewinnen win
gewöhnlich usually
stark **gewürzt** spicy
Gitarre guitar
Glas glass
glauben believe
Glück haben be lucky
glücklich happy
Glückwunsch congratulations
Golf golf
Grad degree
groß big; large; tall
großartig great
Großstadt city
Grube pit
grün green
Gruppe group; band
Gruß greeting
Grüße ausrichten say hello
gut good; well
gut aussehend good-looking
Guten Morgen. Good morning.
gut in good at
Guthaben credit

H

Haar hair
Haare hair
haben have got; have
Haft detention
Hähnchen chicken
halb *(Uhrzeit)* half past
Hallo. Hello; Hi.
Haltestelle station
Hand hand
Handy mobile phone; mobile
hart hard
hassen hate
Haus house
nach Hause home
Hausaufgaben homework
Häuschen cottage

Hausmeister/Hausmeisterin caretaker
Haustier pet
He! Hey!
Heavy Metal heavy metal
Heft book
Heim home
Heimspiel home game
heiraten marry
heiß hot
heißen mean
Ich heiße .... My name is ....
Wie heißt du? What's your name?
heiter sunny
helfen help
Hemd shirt
Henne hen
Jetzt aber **her damit**. Just give it to me.
herausfinden find out
Herbst autumn
Herr Mr *(Anrede)*
herunter down
herunterladen download
heute today
heute Abend tonight
heute Nachmittag this afternoon
heute Nacht tonight
Hexe witch
hier here
Hier bitte. Here you are.
Hier ist Barbara. It's Barbara.
Hier spricht .... This is ... speaking.
Hier ist .... This is ... speaking.
hinauf up
Hindu Hindu
hinduistisch Hindu
hinein into
hineintun put
hinter behind
hinunter down
hinzufügen add
Hit hit
Hobby hobby
hoch high; tall; up
Hochwasser flood
Hochzeit wedding
Hockey hockey
hoffen hope
holen fetch
hören listen to; hear
Hose trousers
Hosentasche pocket
Hotel hotel
hübsch pretty
Hubschrauber helicopter
Huhn hen; chicken
Hülle cover
Hund dog
hundemüde dog-tired
hundert one hundred; a hundred
hungrig hungry
Hut hat
Hütte cottage

I

ich I; me
ich selbst myself
Ich bin's. It's me.
Ich bin .... I'm ....
Ich heiße .... My name is ....
Ich komme aus .... I'm from ....
Ich möchte .... I'd like to ....
Ich würde gerne .... I'd like to ....
ideal ideal
Idee idea
ihm him
ihn him
ihnen them
ihr you
ihr/ihre her; their
Ihr/Ihre your
im in
im Internet on the internet
im Zug on the train
Imbiss snack
immer always
in in; at; into
in der Nähe von near
in der Sendung on the programme
in der Stadt in town
in Form fit
ins Bett gehen go to bed
in Ordnung OK; fine
indisch Indian
Information information
Informationszentrum Information Centre
Inliner in-line skates
Inline-Skates in-line skates
Instrument instrument
interessant interesting
interessiert sein an be interested in
Internet internet
im Internet on the internet
Interview interview
irgendeiner/irgendeine/irgendein any
irgendetwas anything
irgendjemand anybody
irgendwelche any
ist is
... ist hinter dir her ... is after you

J

ja yes; yeah
Jackentasche pocket
Jahr year
Jahrmarkt fair
Januar January
Jazz jazz
Jeans jeans
jeder/jede/jedes every
jeder everybody
jeder (beliebige) anybody
jemals ever
jemand somebody
jemanden erinnern remind somebody
jemand einen Streich spielen play a trick on somebody
jene those
jener/jene/jenes that
jetzt now
Jetzt aber her damit. Just give it to me.
joggen gehen go jogging
Joghurt yoghurt
Journalist/Journalistin journalist
Jugendherberge youth hostel
Juli July
jung young
Junge boy
Juni June

K

Kaffee coffee
Kaffee trinken have a coffee
kalt cold
Kamera camera
kämpfen fight
Kaninchen rabbit
Kapitel unit
kaputt broken
Karaoke karaoke
Karate karate
Karneval carnival
Karotte carrot
Kartentrick card trick
Kartoffel potato
Käse cheese
Katastrophe disaster
Katze cat
kaufen buy; get
Kebab kebab
kein/keine no; not ... any
keiner nobody
kennen know
kennen lernen meet
Schön dich kennen zu lernen. Nice to meet you.
Kerker dungeon

Kilometer kilometre
Kinder children
Kinderschminken face painting
Kino cinema
Kirche church
Kiste box
Klasse tutor group; class
Klasse sieben Year 7
Klassenarbeit test
Klassenzimmer classroom
klassisch classical
Kleid dress
Kleider clothes
Kleidung clothes
klein small
Kleintransporter van
klettern climb
klicken click
klingeln ring
Klingelton ring tone
klug clever
Knopf button
kochen cook
Kohlenbergwerk coal mine
Kohlengrube coal mine
komisch funny
kommen come
Ich komme aus .... I'm from ....
kommen aus come from
Woher kommst du? Where are you from?
Kommunikation communication
König king
Königin queen
können can; may
konnte/konnten could
könnte/könnten could
konnte nicht/konnten nicht couldn't
kontrollieren check
Kontrollliste checklist
Konzert concert
koordinieren organize
Kopf head
kosten cost
Es kostet .... It's ....
Sie kosten .... They're ....
Wie viel kosten sie? How much are they?
Wie viel kostet es? How much is it?
kostenlos free
krank ill
Krankenpfleger nurse
Krankenschwester nurse
Kredit credit
Kricket cricket
kriegen get
Kriminalbeamter/ Kriminalbeamtin detective
Kriminalroman detective story
Küche kitchen
Kuchen cake
Küchenschrank cupboard
Kuh cow
Kunst art
kurz short
Küste coast

L

lachen laugh
laden put
Laden shop
Lage situation
Land country
landen land
Landkarte map
landwirtschaftliche Maschine farm machine
lang long
langsam slow, slowly
langweilig boring
Laptop laptop
Lärm noise
lassen leave
lass/lasst uns let's
Lass mich in Ruhe Leave me alone.
Laterne lantern
laufen walk; run
laut loud, loudly
Laut sound
läuten ring
leben live; be alive
am **Leben sein** be alive
legen put
Lego lego
Lehrer/Lehrerin teacher
leicht easy
Tut mir **Leid**. I'm sorry.
Leine line
leise quiet
lernen learn
lernen über find out about
lesen read
Noten lesen read music
letzter/letzte/letztes last
Leute people
Lieber/Liebe/Liebes *(in Briefanrede)* Dear
Liebe love
lieben love
Lieblings- favourite
Lied song
Liedtext lyrics
Lieferwagen van
Lineal ruler
Linie line
Link link
links left; on the left
Liste list
Löffel spoon
Luft air
Luftballon balloon
lustig funny

M

machen do; make
einen Ausflug machen go on a trip
eine Reise machen go on a trip
ein Foto machen take a picture
macht/machen Spaß is/are fun
Mädchen girl
Magazin magazine
Mahlzeit meal
Mai May
Mama mum
man you
manchmal sometimes
Mann man pl. men
Mannschaft team
Markt market
März March
Mathematik Maths
Maus mouse
Mäuse mice
Meerschweinchen guinea pig
mehr more
mein/meine my
meinen think
Meister/Meisterin champion
Menschen people
merkwürdig strange
Messer knife pl. knives
Meter metre
Methode way
mich me
mich selbst myself
Milch milk
Million million
Mine mine; pit
Minute minute
mir me
Missgeburt freak
mit with
mit dem Bus by bus
mit ... zusammen with
Mitnahmerestaurant takeaway
mitnehmen take
Essen zum Mitnehmen takeaway
zu **Mittag essen** have lunch
Mittagessen lunch
Mittagspause lunch break
Mitteilung message

Mittwoch Wednesday
Mobiltelefon mobile phone
Möchtest du ... ?/Möchten Sie ... ? Would you like ... ?
Modell model
modern modern
mögen want (to); enjoy; like; fancy
Einen **Moment** bitte. Just a minute, please.
Monat month
Monster monster
Montag Monday
morgen tomorrow
Morgen morning
morgens in the morning
am Morgen in the morning
Guten Morgen. Good morning.
MP3 Player MP3 player
müde tired
Museum museum
Musik music
müssen must; have to
Muster design
Mutter mother

N

nach to; after; past
nach Hause home
nach unten down
Nachbildung model
Nachmittag afternoon
Nachricht message
Nachsitzen detention
nächster/nächste/nächstes next
nächstes Mal next time
Nacht night
nahe near
in der **Nähe von** near
Nahrung food; diet
Name name
nass wet
Nationalität nationality
Natur nature
natürlich of course
Naturwissenschaft Science
neben next to
nehmen take
nein no
nervös nervous
nett nice
Netz web; network
Netzwerk web; network
neu new
nicht not
konnte nicht/konnten nicht couldn't
nicht dürfen mustn't
nicht können can't
nicht mögen hate
nicht werden won't
nichts not ... anything
nie never
niemals never
niemand nobody
noch still; yet
noch einmal again
noch nicht not yet
noch einer/eine/eins another
Norden north
normalerweise usually
Norwegisch Norwegian
Note grade
Noten lesen read music
Notizen notes
Notizen machen take notes
November November
Nudeln pasta
null oh
Nummer number
nun now
nun (ja) well
nur only; just

O

ob if
oberer Teil top
Obst fruit
oder or
offen open
öffnen open
oft often
Oh. Oh.
ohne without
Ohrring earring
OK OK
Oktober October
Oma grandma
Onkel uncle
online online
Opa grandad
Orangensaft orange juice
Orchester orchestra
ordentlich tidy
organisieren organize
Ort place
Osten east

P

packen pack
Palast palace
Papa dad
Park park
Parkplatz car park
Partner partner
Party party
eine Party feiern have a party
passieren happen
Pause break
peinlich embarrassing
peinlicher more embarrassing
der/die/das **peinlichste** the most embarrassing
Pence *(britische Währungseinheit)* penny pl. pence
Person person
Pfad path
Pfund *(britische Währungseinheit)* pound
Pilot/Pilotin pilot
pink pink
Pizza pizza
Plan plan
planen plan
Plappermaul chatterbox
Platz place; position
plötzlich suddenly
Polizei police pl. police
Polizist/Polizistin police officer
Pommes frites chips
Pony pony
Popkonzert pop concert
Popstar pop star
populär popular
Porträt profile
Posaune trombone
Position position
Postamt post office
Poster poster
Postkarte postcard
Präsentation presentation
präsentieren present
Preis prize
prima cool
Prinzessin princess
privat private
pro per
Problem problem
Profil profile
Programm plan
Projekt project
Projekttag project day
prüfen check
Publikumssport spectator sport
Punkt point
Puzzle jigsaw puzzle

Q

Quiz quiz

R

Radiergummi rubber

Radio radio
Ratschlag tip
Rätsel puzzle
Raum room
Rechnung bill
Recht haben be right
rechts right; on the right
Rechtschreibung spelling
reden talk
reden mit talk to
reden über talk about
Regel rule
Regen rain
regnen rain
regnerisch rainy
Reihenfolge order
Reis rice
Reise trip
eine Reise machen go on a trip
reiten ride
Rektor/Rektorin headteacher
rennen run
Rennen race
reparieren repair
Reporter/Reporterin reporter
Restaurant restaurant
Resultat result
retten save
richtig right
riesig large
Roboter robot
Rock skirt
rosa pink
rot red
Route route
Rucksack rucksack
Ruderclub rowing club
rudern gehen go rowing
rufen call; shout
ruhig quiet

S

Sache thing
sagen say; tell
Salat salad
Samstag Saturday
Sandwich sandwich
Sänger/Sängerin singer
Sanktion sanction
Satz sentence
sauber tidy
Schach chess
Schachtel box
Es ist **schade.** It's a pity.
Schaf sheep pl. sheep
Schaltfläche button
scharf spicy
schauen look
schenken give
scheußlich awful
schicken send, sent, sent
schieben push
schießen kick
Schiff boat; ship
Schild, Zeichen sign
schlafen sleep
schlafen gehen go to bed
Schlafsack sleeping bag
Schlafzimmer bedroom
Schlagzeile headline
Schlagzeug drums
schlecht bad
schlechter worse
der/die/das **schlechteste** the worst
schließen close
schlimm bad
schlimmer worse
der/die/das **schlimmste** the worst
schlittschuhlaufen gehen go ice skating
Schloss castle
Schluss end; ending
Schluss machen break up
schmerzen hurt
schmerzlich sad
Schnee snow
schnell quick; fast
schockiert shocked
Schokolade chocolate
schön nice
Schön dich kennen zu lernen. Nice to meet you.
schon yet; already
schottisch Scottish
Schrank cupboard
schreiben write
Schreib zurück (SZ). Text me back.
eine SMS schreiben text
schreien shout; scream
Schritt step
Schuh shoe
Schule school
Schüler/Schülerin pupil
Schulfach subject
Schulfest fair
Schulklasse class
Schulleiter/Schulleiterin headteacher
Schulmannschaft school team
Schulstunde lesson
Schuppen shed
Schwamm sponge
schwarz black
schwarzes Brett board
Schwein pig
Schwester sister
schwierig hard; difficult
Schwierigkeiten trouble
Schwimmbad swimming pool
Schwimmbecken swimming pool
schwimmen swim
schwimmen gehen go swimming
Schwimmer/Schwimmerin swimmer
See lake
sehen see; look
Wir sehen uns dort. See you there.
Sehenswürdigkeit sight
sehr very
seid are
Seil line
sein be
Sei/Seid leise. Be quiet.
sein/seine his
Seite page
selbst herself; himself; themselves; myself; ourselves; yourself
selbstverständlich of course
seltsam strange
Semester term
senden send
Sendung programme
in der Sendung on the programme
September September
setzen put
sich anschließen join
sich ausdenken make up
sich beruhigen relax
sich erinnern remember
sich fühlen feel
sich interessieren für be interested in
sich prügeln fight
sich selbst herself; himself; themselves
sich treffen meet
sich trennen split; break up
sich verlaufen get lost
sicher sure
sie she; they; them; her
Sie kosten ... . They're ... .
sie selbst herself; themselves
Simulator simulator
sind are
singen sing
Situation situation
sitzen sit
Skateboard skateboard
Ski ski
SMS text message
eine SMS schreiben text
Snack snack
so so
soeben just
Sofa sofa

Sohn son
sollte besser/sollten besser ought to
sollte/sollten should
du solltest you should
Sommer summer
sonderbar strange
sonnig sunny
Sonntag Sunday
sonntags on Sunday
am Sonntag on Sunday
Sonst noch etwas? Anything else?
sorgfältig careful
Viel **Spaß!** Have fun!
spät late
Speicher attic
Spiel game; play
spielen play
spielen (eine Rolle) act
jemand einen Streich spielen play a trick on somebody
Spieler/Spielerin player
Spinne spider
Spitze top
Sport sports
Sport(arten) treiben do sports
Sportplatz sports field
Sportunterricht PE
Sprache language
Sprachmittlung mediation
sprechen speak; talk
sprechen mit talk to
sprechen über talk about
Sprecher speaker
springen jump
Sprungschanze ski jump
Staatsangehörigkeit nationality
Stadt town; city
in der Stadt in town
Stadtplan map
Stadtzentrum town centre
Stand stall
Star star
stark gewürzt spicy
stecken put
stehen stand
stehlen steal
Stelle place
stellen put
sterben die
Stern star
Stier bull
Stil style
Stimme voice
stinkend smelly
stoßen push
Strafe sanction
Strand beach
Straße road; street
Strecke route
jemand einen **Streich spielen** play a trick on somebody
streiten argue
streng strict
Stress stress
Strichmännchen matchstick man
Stuhl chair
Stunde hour
Stundenplan timetable
Sturm storm
suchen look for
Süden south
Südwest- southwest
südwestlich southwest
super awesome
surfen surf
surfen gehen go surfing
Surfen surfing
süß cute
Sweatshirt sweatshirt

T

Tafel board
Tag day
Tal valley
tanzen dance
Tänzer/Tänzerin dancer
Tasche bag
Taschenlampe torch
Tasse cup
Tätigkeit activity
tauschen exchange
tausend one thousand
Taxi taxi
Team team
Tee tea
Teich pond
Teigwaren pasta
Teil part
teilnehmen an take part in
Telefon telephone; phone
Telefongespräch phone call
Telefonzelle phone box
Tempel temple
Temperatur temperature
Tennis tennis
Test test
teuer expensive
Text text
Theaterstück play
Thema topic
Ticket ticket
Tier animal
Tipp tip
Tisch table
Titel title
Titelseite cover
Toast(brot) toast
Tochter daughter
Toilette toilet
toll fantastic
Ton sound
Tor gate
Tornado tornado
tot dead
total totally
Tour tour
Tourist/Touristin tourist
tragen carry; wear *(Kleidung)*
Trainer coach
trainieren train
Training training
Traktor tractor
traurig sad
treffen meet
Treffpunkt meeting place
Treppe stairs
treten kick
Trick trick
Trimester term
trinken drink
Trompete trumpet
T-Shirt T-shirt
tun do; make
Tunnel tunnel
Tür door
Turm tower
Turnhalle sports hall
Turnier competition
Turnschuh trainer
Tut mir Leid. I'm sorry.
Typ type
tyrannisieren bully

U

U-Bahn Underground
üben practise
über over; about
übernachten stay
Überschrift title
Überschwemmung flood
Übung exercise
Übungsheft exercise book
Uhr clock
... Uhr ... o'clock
Wie viel Uhr ist es? What time is it?
um at
um zu to
Umfrage survey
Umkleideraum changing room
umsteigen nach change to
Umzug procession
unangenehm embarrassing
unangenehmer more embarrassing
der/die/das **unangenehmste** the most embarrassing

und and
Unfall accident
ungefähr about
Ungeheuer monster
Unglück disaster
unglücklich unhappy
Uniform uniform
Unrecht haben be wrong
uns us
uns selbst ourselves
unser/unsere our
unter under
Unterführung tunnel
unterrichten teach
Unterrichtsstunde lesson
Urlaub holiday

V

Vater father
Vegetarier/Vegetarierin vegetarian
vegetarisch vegetarian
verängstigt sein be scared
veranstalten organize
Veranstaltung event
verbinden join
Verbindung link
Verbrecher/Verbrecherin criminal
Verein club
verfehlen miss
... verfolgt dich ... is after you
vergessen forget
verkaufen sell
verlassen leave
verlieren lose
Verlies dungeon
vermissen miss
verpassen miss
verregnet rainy
verrückt crazy
verschieden different
verschwistert twinned
verstehen understand
versuchen try
verwenden use
Vetter cousin
Videokamera video camera
viel much
Viel Spaß! Have fun!
viele lots of; many
vielleicht maybe
viertel nach quarter past
Vogel bird
Volksfest carnival
Volleyball volleyball
völlig totally
von from; of; by
von ... bis from ... to
vor ago; in front of; to
Vordruck form
vorhaben going to
Vormittag morning
vorne at the front
vorsichtig careful
Vorsingen audition
Vorspielen audition
vorstellen present
vorziehen prefer

W

Wachfrau security guard
Wachmann security guard
wahr true
während during
wahrscheinlich probably
Waliser/Waliserin Welsh
walisisch Welsh
Wand wall
wann when
warm warm
warten wait
warten auf wait for
warum why
was what
Was fehlt? What's missing?
Was geht hier vor? What's happening?
Was ist los? What's wrong?; What's the matter?
waschen wash
Wasser water
Website website
wechseln exchange
weg away
Weg path; way
wegen about
weglaufen vor run from
wehtun hurt
weil because
weiß white
weitergehen go on
weitermachen go on
Weitsprung long jump
welcher/welche/welches what; which
Welche Farbe hat ... ? What colour is ... ?
wenn when; if
wer who
werden will; going to; get
werfen throw
Westen west
westindisch; Westinder/Westinderin West Indian
Wettbewerb competition
Wetter weather
Wettkampf competition
wichtig important
wie like; as; how
wie viel how much
Wie alt bist du? How old are you?
Wie geht's? How are you?
Wie heißt du? What's your name?
Wie ist ... ? What's ... like?
wie viele how many
Wie viel kosten sie? How much are they?
Wie viel kostet es? How much is it?
Wie viel Uhr ist es? What time is it?
wieder again
Wikinger Viking
wild wild
willkommen welcome
Wind wind
Winter winter
wir we; us
wir selbst ourselves
Wir sehen uns dort. See you there.
wirklich really
wissen know
wissen von know about
Wissenschaft Science
Witz joke
wo where
Woche week
Wochenende weekend
am Wochenende at the weekend
Woher kommst du? Where are you from?
wohin where
wohnen live; stay
Wohnung flat
Wohnzimmer living room
wolkig cloudy
wollen want (to)
Wort word
Wörterbuch dictionary
wütend angry

Y

Yoga yoga

Z

Zahl number
zahlen pay
Zeichen sign
Zeichentrickfilm cartoon
zeichnen draw
zeigen show
Zeile line

Zeit time
die Zeiten messen take the times
Zeitschrift magazine
Zeitung newspaper
Zelt tent
Zeltplatz campsite
zerbrechen break
zerstören destroy
Zeugnis report; profile
ziehen pull
ziemlich quite
Zimmer room
Zimmer mit Frühstück bed and breakfast (B & B)
Zoo zoo
zornig angry
zu too; to; about
zu Hause at home
zu spät late
Zucker sugar
zuerst first
Zug train
Zuhause home
zuhören listen
Zukunft future
zuordnen match
zurück back
zusammen together
zusammenpassen go together
zusammenpassen mit go with
Zusatz extra
zusätzlich extra
Zuschauer/Zuschauerin spectator
zusehen watch
zwischen between

Check the answers!

Revision 1-4

1 Questions and answers
2. I could show you the London Eye. 3. No, you ought to wear nice clothes. 4. You can take the Underground. 5. No, I haven't. My old one is OK. 6. I'm not sure. I'll ask my mum first. 7. I went shopping and forgot to call you. 8. Let's meet in the new café. It's cool!

2 Good tips
1. mustn't 2. ought to 3. mustn't 4. must 5. ought to 6. must 7. mustn't 8. ought to

3 Did you forget ...?
A: Did you forget our meeting yesterday?
B: Yes, I did. I'm sorry.
A: Where were you?
B: I was at the market.
A: Did you like it? Did you buy anything?
B: It was very cool. I bought a nice present for a friend.
A: What? I don't want to see you again.
B: I'm sorry! Let's talk about it tomorrow.
A: Goodbye!
B: Goodbye.

4 The wrong word
1. driver 2. France 3. listen to it 4. awful 5. message 6. topic

5 How can you do it?
b) 1. run: well, quickly, angrily, ...
2. dance: well, happily, crazily, ...
3. shout: loudly, angrily, ...
4. draw: nicely, beautifully, slowly, ...
5. eat: quickly, slowly, ...
6. sing: loudly, well, quietly, ...
7. play the guitar: nicely, badly, loudly, ...
8. play football: well, badly, quickly, happily, ...

Revision 5-8

1 Questions and answers
2. You can take a flight. 3. We'd like to climb Ben Nevis. 4. We'd like to stay in a cottage. 5. Yes, we went there last year. 6. I totally love DJ Dan! 7. If it's sunny, we'll go swimming. 8. Well, I like darts.

2 We haven't done it yet!
2. Tom hasn't been to London yet. 3. Look, I've found some money in the street. 4. Sorry, I've just broken Grandma's expensive cup. 5. We haven't seen Nessie yet. 6. Sorry, I haven't done my homework yet.

3 Myself, yourself, ...
2. myself 3. herself, himself 4. themselves 5. ourselves 6. yourselves

4 If ...
2. If it's sunny tomorrow, we'll go swimming. 3. But if it rains, we won't go to the beach. 4. If Tom doesn't train more, he'll lose the next race, too. 5. If you don't visit us this evening, I won't see you again before the holidays.

5 Peter Robbins
play, orchestra, practise, loudly, nervous, singer, voice, meet, listen to, download, internet, understands, important, song

6 Andrew
a) Andrew always watches Formula One races on TV. They are really exciting, but also very dangerous.

7 What is it?
Beispiellösungen:
2. This means that you take things from the internet. 3. This is somebody that is not very active. 4. This is the Scottish word for lake. 5. This is a place where you can stay. 6. With a trombone you can make music. 7. You can see this in winter. It's cold and white.

Irregular verbs

Diese Liste enthält alle unregelmäßigen Verben, die in Let's go *vorkommen. Sie enthält jeweils alle drei Formen, auch wenn sie nicht alle im Text erscheinen.*

Verb	Vergangenheit	Perfekt	Auf Deutsch
be	was, were	been	*sein*
break	broke	broken	*(zer)brechen*
buy	bought	bought	*kaufen*
come	came	come	*kommen*
cost	cost	cost	*kosten*
do	did	done	*tun, machen*
draw	drew	drawn	*zeichnen*
drink	drank	drunk	*trinken*
drive	drove	driven	*fahren*
eat	ate	eaten	*essen*
fall	fell	fallen	*fallen*
feed	fed	fed	*füttern*
feel	felt	felt	*(sich) fühlen*
fight	fought	fought	*kämpfen*
find	found	found	*finden*
fly	flew	flown	*fliegen*
forget	forgot	forgotten	*vergessen*
get	got	got	*bekommen, werden*
give	gave	given	*geben*
go	went	gone	*gehen, fahren*
have	had	had	*haben*
hear	heard	heard	*hören*
hurt	hurt	hurt	*wehtun, schmerzen*
know	knew	known	*kennen, wissen*
leave	left	left	*(ver)lassen*
lose	lost	lost	*verlieren*
make	made	made	*machen, tun*
mean	meant	meant	*bedeuten*
meet	met	met	*(sich) treffen*
pay	paid	paid	*(be)zahlen*
put	put	put	*stellen, legen, setzen*
read	read	read	*lesen*
ride	rode	ridden	*reiten, fahren*
ring	rang	rung	*klingeln, anrufen*
run	ran	run	*rennen, laufen*
say	said	said	*sagen*
see	saw	seen	*sehen*
sell	sold	sold	*verkaufen*
send	sent	sent	*schicken*
sing	sang	sung	*singen*
sit	sat	sat	*sitzen*
sleep	slept	slept	*schlafen*
speak	spoke	spoken	*sprechen*
split	split	split	*sich trennen*
stand	stood	stood	*stehen*

Verb	Vergangenheit	Perfekt	Auf Deutsch
steal	stole	stolen	*stehlen*
swim	swam	swum	*schwimmen*
take	took	taken	*bringen, nehmen*
teach	taught	taught	*unterrichten*
tell	told	told	*sagen, erzählen*
think	thought	thought	*denken*
throw	threw	thrown	*werfen*
understand	understood	understood	*verstehen*
wear	wore	worn	*tragen, anhaben*
win	won	won	*gewinnen*
write	wrote	written	*schreiben*

Numbers

0 = nought, zero
1 = one
2 = two
3 = three
4 = four
5 = five
6 = six
7 = seven
8 = eight
9 = nine
10 = ten
11 = eleven
12 = twelve
13 = thirteen
14 = fourteen
15 = fifteen
16 = sixteen
17 = seventeen
18 = eighteen
19 = nineteen

20 = twenty
21 = twenty-one
22 = twenty-two
30 = thirty
40 = forty
50 = fifty
60 = sixty
70 = seventy
80 = eighty
90 = ninety
100 = one/a hundred
101 = one/a hundred **and** one
202 = two hundred **and** two
303 = three hundred **and** three
1,000 = one/a thousand
1,004 = one/a thousand **and** four
2,000 = two thousand
2,005 = two thousand **and** five
3,500 = three thousand five hundred
1,000,000 = one million

In the classroom

Dies ist eine Liste der wichtigsten Arbeitsanweisungen in Let's go.
Deine Lehrerin oder dein Lehrer benutzt sie, wenn du etwas tun sollst:

Act the dialogue with a partner.	*Spiele das Gespräch mit einem Partner.*
Answer the questions.	*Beantworte die Fragen.*
Ask a friend/a partner.	*Frage einen Freund/einen Partner.*
Can you find the numbers?	*Kannst du die Zahlen finden?*
Come to the board, please.	*Komm bitte an die Tafel.*
Go on, please.	*Mach bitte weiter.*
Is that right?	*Ist das richtig?*
Listen and speak.	*Höre zu und sprich nach.*
Look at the pictures.	*Schau dir die Bilder an.*
Listen carefully to the dialogues.	*Höre dir die Dialoge genau an.*
Make a word web.	*Mache ein Wortnetz.*
Make dialogues with a partner.	*Mache Dialoge mit einem Partner.*
Match the names with the dates.	*Ordne die Namen den Daten zu.*
Match the parts of the sentences.	*Ordne die Satzteile einander zu.*
Open your books at page 15.	*Schlagt eure Bücher auf Seite 15 auf.*
Put the words in different groups.	*Ordne die Wörter verschiedenen Gruppen zu.*
Read the sentences.	*Lies die Sätze.*
Right or wrong?	*Richtig oder falsch?*
Say it in English.	*Sag es auf Englisch.*
Take notes.	*Mache dir Notizen.*
Think of something new.	*Denk dir etwas Neues aus.*
What can you see in the picture?	*Was siehst du auf dem Bild?*
What colour is it?	*Welche Farbe hat er/sie/es?*
What's missing?	*Was fehlt?*
What's the right order?	*Was ist die richtige Reihenfolge?*
What's the right word?	*Was ist das richtige Wort?*
Who is it?	*Wer ist es?*
Work in groups and do a presentation.	*Arbeitet in Gruppen und erstellt eine Präsentation.*
Write a short text in English.	*Schreibe einen kurzen Text auf Englisch.*

Das kannst du sagen, wenn du etwas tun möchtest oder ein Problem hast:

Can I go outside, please?	*Darf ich bitte hinausgehen?*
Can I go to the toilet, please?	*Kann ich bitte auf die Toilette gehen?*
Can I open the window, please?	*Kann ich bitte das Fenster aufmachen?*
Can I work with …?	*Kann ich mit … zusammenarbeiten?*
Can we sing a song/play a game?	*Können wir ein Lied singen/ein Spiel machen?*
Can you help me, please?	*Können Sie/Kannst du mir bitte helfen?*
I don't understand this.	*Ich verstehe das hier nicht.*
Pardon?	*Wie bitte?*
Sorry, I haven't got my homework.	*Entschuldigung, ich habe meine Hausaufgaben nicht.*
What's that in German?	*Wie heißt das auf Deutsch?*

Das kannst du sagen, wenn du mit dem Computer arbeitest:

Have you got an e-mail address?	*Hast du eine E-Mail-Adresse?*
What's the address of this website?	*Wie ist die Adresse dieser Webseite?*
Click on this link here.	*Klicke diesen Link an.*
How can I surf the internet?	*Wie kann ich im Internet surfen?*
I can't understand this message.	*Ich verstehe diese Nachricht nicht.*
It won't accept my username/password.	*Mein Benutzername/Passwort wird nicht akzeptiert.*
Can I download it/print it out?	*Kann ich es herunterladen/ausdrucken?*
How can I burn it onto a CD?	*Wie kann ich es auf CD brennen?*
My computer has crashed.	*Mein Computer ist abgestürzt.*
What do I type in here?	*Was muss ich hier eingeben?*

Quellen

Bildquellen:
Umschlag: 1: Mauritius (Merten), Mittenwald; S. 2: Avenue Images GmbH (Stockbyte Gold), Hamburg; U2.1: London Transport Museum, London; S. 3.1: mecom (ddp / Gerhard Blank), Hamburg; S. 8.1: www.britainonview.com, London; S. 8.2: Klett-Archiv (Hacker), Stuttgart; S. 8.3: Mauritius (age), Mittenwald; S. 9.1: Picture-Alliance, Frankfurt; S. 9.2: Corbis (Kim Sayer), Düsseldorf; S. 11.1: Klett-Archiv (Hacker), Stuttgart; S. 15.1: NewsCast, London; S. 17.1: CartoonStock (Mike Mittelstadt), Bath; S. 20.1: Picture-Alliance (Heiko Wolfraum), Frankfurt; S. 20.2: Getty Images (taxi / Erin Patrice O'Brien), München; S. 21.1: Mauritius (A. Mayer), Mittenwald; S. 21.2: Klett-Archiv (Hacker), Stuttgart; S. 21.3: Getty Images (taxi / Denis Felix), München; S. 21.4: Picture-Alliance (Frank May), Frankfurt; S. 22.1: Siemens AG, München; S. 23.1: Getty Images (Photodisc), München; S. 23.2: Avenue Images GmbH (image 100), Hamburg; S. 23.3: Avenue Images GmbH (Digital Vision), Hamburg; S. 23.4: Bananastock RF, Watlington / Oxon; S. 24.1: Klett-Archiv (Fletcher), Stuttgart; S. 24.2: Modular (Steinle), Stuttgart; S. 25.1: Argum (Christian Lehsten), München; S. 26.1: Picture-Alliance (ZB), Frankfurt; S. 26.2: Alamy Images RM (Jeff Morgan), Abingdon, Oxon; S. 27.1: Corel Corporation, Ottawa, Ontario; S. 27.2: Alamy Images RM (Photolibrary Wales), Abingdon, Oxon; S. 27.3: Alamy Images RM (Photolibrary Wales), Abingdon, Oxon; S. 27.4: Avenue Images GmbH (Comstock RF), Hamburg; S. 31.1: Avenue Images GmbH (Brand X RF), Hamburg; S. 35.1: CartoonStock (Geoff McNeill), Bath; S. 35.2: Corbis GmbH (Mark E. Gibson); S. 35.3: Klett-Archiv (Fletcher), Stuttgart; S. 35.4: Fotosearch RF (Design Pics), Waukesha, WI; S. 35.5: Fotosearch RF (Stockbyte), Waukesha, WI; S. 35.6: Alamy Images RM (Jeff Morgan), Abingdon, Oxon; S. 35.7: Getty Images (Image Bank / Alan Thor), München; S. 38.1: Avenue Images GmbH (RF Design Pics), Hamburg; S. 38.2: Alamy Images RM (Photofusion Picture Library), Abingdon, Oxon; S. 39.1: Alamy Images RM (Diomedia), Abingdon, Oxon; S. 40.1: Avenue Images GmbH (RF Design Pics), Hamburg; S. 40.2: Alamy Images RM (Janine Wiedel Photolibrary), Abingdon, Oxon; S. 42.1: Avenue Images GmbH (Image Source), Hamburg; S. 42.2: Avenue Images GmbH (Comstock), Hamburg; S. 46.1: MEV, Augsburg; S. 46.2: Mauritius (Vidler), Mittenwald; S. 46.3: Avenue Images GmbH (image 100), Hamburg; S. 46.4: Alamy Images RM (Photolibrary Wales), Abingdon, Oxon; S. 47.1: Alamy Images RM (colinspics), Abingdon, Oxon; S. 47.2: Alamy Images RM (Photofusion Picture Library), Abingdon, Oxon; S. 47.3: Alamy Images RM (worldthroughthelens), Abingdon, Oxon; S. 52.1: Getty Images (Tony Feder), München; S. 55.1: Alamy Images RM (nagelestock.com), Abingdon, Oxon; S. 58.1: Picture-Alliance (Landov Robert E. Klein), Frankfurt; S. 58.2: Imageshop RF (RF), Düsseldorf; S. 58.3: Picture-Alliance (Yui Mok), Frankfurt; S. 58.4: Fotosearch RF (Brand X Pictures), Waukesha, WI; S. 59.1: Alamy Images Limited (Steve Skjold); S. 59.2: Getty Images (Digital Vision), München; S. 60.1: Corbis (Rune Hellestadt), Düsseldorf; S. 63.1: Fotosearch RF (PhotoDisc), Waukesha, WI; S. 63.2: Fotosearch/Photodisc; S. 63.3: Fotosearch RF (Image 100), Waukesha, WI; S. 64.1: Getty Images (Bruno Vincent), München; S. 64.2: Picture-Alliance (Parsons), Frankfurt; S. 64.3: Schlüter, Heinz, Flensburg; S. 64.4: Corbis (George Hall), Düsseldorf; S. 65.1: Avenue Images GmbH (Digital Vision RF), Hamburg; S. 65.2: Getty Images (Graeme Robertson), München; S. 65.3: Picture-Alliance (Steve Pope), Frankfurt; S. 67.1: Getty Images (stone / Jorn Georg Tornter), München; S. 67.2: Picture-Alliance (Barry Batcher), Frankfurt; S. 71.1: www.jalite.co.uk; S. 73.1: CartoonStock (Robert Thompson), Bath; S. 76.1: Bananastock RF (RF), Watlington / Oxon; S. 76.2: Alamy Images RM (Profimedia.CZ s.r.o.), Abingdon, Oxon; S. 76.3: Getty Images (PhotoDisc), München; S. 76.4: Getty Images (Image Bank / Terje Rakke), München; S. 76.5: Getty Images (Workbook Stock / Mills), München; S. 77.1: Alamy Images RM (Photo Network), Abingdon, Oxon; S. 77.2: Avenue Images GmbH (Rubberball RF), Hamburg; S. 77.3: MEV, Augsburg; S. 77.4: www.britainonview.com, London W6 9EL; S. 80.1: Alamy Images RM (Lisa Battaglene), Abingdon, Oxon; S. 81.1: Klett-Archiv (Smith), Stuttgart; S. 84.1: Getty Images (Photodisc), München; S. 84.2: Alamy Images RM (Alex Segre), Abingdon, Oxon; S. 88.1: Klett-Archiv (Smith), Stuttgart; S. 88.2: Klett-Archiv (Smith), Stuttgart; S. 88.3: Klett-Archiv (Smith), Stuttgart; S. 8.4: Klett-Archiv (Smith), Stuttgart; S. 88.5: Klett-Archiv (Smith), Stuttgart; S. 88.6: Klett-Archiv (Smith), Stuttgart; S. 88.7: Klett-Archiv (Smith), Stuttgart; S. 88.8: Klett-Archiv (Smith), Stuttgart; S. 88.9: Klett-Archiv (Smith), Stuttgart; S. 88.10: Alamy Images RM (oote boe), Abingdon, Oxon; S. 89.1: Klett-Archiv (Smith), Stuttgart; S. 89.2: Klett-Archiv (Smith), Stuttgart; S. 89.3: Corbis (David Ball), Düsseldorf; S. 89.3: Klett-Archiv (Smith), Stuttgart; S. 90.1: Corbis (Roy McMahon), Düsseldorf; S. 90.2: Getty Images (PhotoDisc), München; S. 90.3: MEV, Augsburg

Textquellen:
S. 23: © Happy Mel Boopy's Cocktail Lounge And Music / Zomba Songs Inc., Musik-Edition Discoton GmbH (BMG Music Publ. Germany) München, Ooky Spinalton Music / EMI April Music Inc., EMI Music Publishing Germany GmbH & Co. KG, Hamburg; S. 61: © EMI Music Publishing Germany GmbH & Co KG, Hamburg, Universal Music Publ. GmbH, Berlin; S. 79: © Queen Music Ltd. D / A / CH / Osteuropäische Länder: EMI Music Publishing Germany GmbH, Hamburg; S. 90.1: © 2001 by Kenn Nesbitt. Reprinted from *The Aliens Have Landed!* with permission from Meadowbrook Press; S. 90.2: © 2004 by Matthew M. Fredericks. Reprinted from *If Kids Ruled the School* with permission from Meadowbrook Press

Flags

Match the flags with the countries. You can find the answers on the internet.

Europe

	Country	Adjective
1	Albania	Albanian
2	Austria	Austrian
3	Belarus	Belarusan
4	Belgium	Belgian
5	Bosnia and Herzegovina	Bosnian Herzegovinian
6	Bulgaria	Bulgarian
7	Croatia	Croatian
8	Czech Republic	Czech
9	Denmark	Danish
10	Estonia	Estonian
11	Finland	Finnish
12	France	French
13	Germany	German
14	Greece	Greek
15	Hungary	Hungarian
16	Iceland	Icelandic
17	Ireland	Irish
18	Italy	Italian
19	Latvia	Latvian
20	Lithuania	Lithuanian
21	Luxembourg	Luxembourgish
22	Macedonia	Macedonian
23	Moldova	Moldovan
24	The Netherlands	Dutch
25	Norway	Norwegian
26	Poland	Polish
27	Portugal	Portuguese
28	Romania	Romanian
29	Russia	Russian
30	Serbia and Montenegro	Serbian Montenegrin
31	Slovakia	Slovak
32	Slovenia	Slovenian
33	Spain	Spanish
34	Sweden	Swedish
35	Switzerland	Swiss
36	Turkey	Turkish
37	Ukraine	Ukrainian
38	United Kingdom	British